$ 125 00
set

24 Vol.

This book was once tied to these information sources:
www.thousandyearoldvampire.com and dearleadergame@gmail.com.

If the above contact methods do not work
simply write your letter on a piece of salted paper
and bury it under a pile of still steaming fulgurite.
Shout "No gods, no masters" at the moon
to complete the procedure.

I will find your message.

This book is dedicated to my wife and child without
who it would never have been completed.

Credits, fonts, and commendations appear
in Appendix VIII of this book.

begun 2018, completed 2019, first distributed in 2020
this is the fifth printing, 2023

Printed in the U.S.A.
©2019 Petit Guignol LLC and Tim Hutchings.

Thousand Year Old Vampire

a game by
Tim Hutchings

ruc

the third section

Under the
bridges of
Paris

ricricricricricricricr
ricricricricricricricr
ricricric

Thousand Year Old Vampire

Thousand Year Old Vampire is a lonely solo role-playing game in which you chronicle the unlife of a vampire over the many centuries of their existence, beginning with the loss of mortality and ending with their inevitable destruction. This vampire will surprise you as they do things that are unexpected, unpleasant, and sometimes tragic. Making gut-churning decisions, performing irreconcilable acts, and resolving difficult narrative threads are what this game is about as you explore the vampire's human failings, villainous acts, and surprising victories.

Game mechanics are simple and intuitive. Play progresses semi-randomly through the Prompts section of this book. Answer Prompts to learn about your vampire's wants and needs, to learn what challenges they face, and to chart their decline into senescence. Build up a character record of Memories and then lose them to the inexorable crush of time. See everyone you've loved and hated grow old and die, then turn to dust.

While playing this game you will encounter themes of death, selfishness, and predation. Your character may be injured, victimized, trapped, or killed. Your character will murder and victimize people of all sorts, possibly including children, animals, loved ones, marginalized people, or themselves. You might find yourself exploring themes of imperialism, colonialism, or oppression. Characters might engage in self-harm or drug abuse. Illness, debilitation, and body horror may come into play. Your character may have their memories altered, they will certainly forget important things.

Some of this will emerge from the Prompts, some will emerge from the choices you make as a player.

This is a personal, challenging game for mature adults. Please play hard, but stay aware of yourself and your feelings. Some good thoughts about safety in solo games can be found in Appendix Three.

What is needed to play?

You will need a ten-sided die (d10) and a six-sided die (d6). If you lack dice, there are random number tables in Appendix II. To use them, all you need to do is drop a coin, point a finger, or use some other method to choose a random number from the table.

You will also need a way to record your vampire's story. Paper and pencil is fine, though it is very convenient to use a word processing document or other digital text tool. In a quick game you only need a few pieces of paper to maintain a character record but in the journaling game you might fill a whole diary. If you are brave or foolish, you can write in this book in the spaces provided.

In the appendix you will also find multiplayer rules, safety tools which let you push yourself as hard as possible, alternate Prompts, examples of play, and some context for the creation of the game itself.

Your Vampire

The vampire whose chronicles you will record in this game is represented by five different traits:

Memories
Skills
Resources
Characters
Marks

Almost every time you receive a **Prompt**, one of your traits will be modified. For instance, you may be instructed to check a Skill.

To do so, you place a checkmark next to that Skill. Alternately, the Prompt may cause you to lose a trait, which is indicated by striking it out with a line. Ensure that the lost trait stays readable because you may refer back to it later or even restore it. Some Prompts will give even more dramatic instructions for changing your traits. At all times, follow the instructions given in the Prompt.

Santa Carla County
Free Library

iii

Memories

Memories and **Experiences** are important moments that have shaped your vampire, crystallized in writing. They make up the core of the vampire's self—the things they know and care about. An Experience is a particular event; a Memory is an arc of Experiences that are tied together by subject or theme.

Experiences cover a particular event, but the amount of time represented by that event might vary dramatically. An Experience might describe a few seconds of impactful events, or it might cover two hundred years of lurking in an old castle.

Almost every Prompt will create an Experience, and Experiences eventually combine with one another to become Memories. But there is only so much your vampire can remember. To reflect this limitation there is only a finite amount of space for Memories on your record sheet. Old Memories will be lost over the course of the game, making

room for new ones. You will need to make difficult choices about which Memories to preserve and which to forget; these hard decisions are the core of the game.

In game terms, an Experience is a single sentence that describes the resolution of a Prompt. Memories are a collection of related Experiences built up over time. Your vampire begins the game with space for five Memories, each of which can contain up to three Experiences.

Although a Prompt might ask several questions, an Experience does not need to address all of them.

An Experience should be a single evocative sentence. An Experience is the distillation of an event—a single sentence that combines what happened and why it matters to your vampire. A good format for an Experience is "[description of the event]; [how I feel or what I did about it]." If necessary, you can add an em dash at the end to include more information.

Be conscious of any traits affected by the Prompt, such as Characters or Resources, and try to incorporate them. Write in the first-person, from the vampire's point of view.

One vampire might have the following Experience:

Stalking the deserts over lonely years, I watch generations of Christian knights waste themselves on the swords of the Saracen; it's a certainty that Charles is among them—I dream of his touch as I sleep beneath the burning sand.

Memories are made up of Experiences. A Memory is a section of the record sheet that contains up to three Experiences. Memories are not necessarily linear or chronological. If a new Experience clearly belongs within an existing Memory, then you can add it to that Memory. If not, record the Experience in a new

Memory, which may require the forgetting of an earlier Memory—a whole collection of other Experiences.

A Memory is a container for Experiences that are related in some way.

An Experience must be placed within a Memory as soon as it is created.

Our earlier example might be expanded with a second Experience like this:

Stalking the deserts over lonely years, I watch generations of Christian knights waste themselves on the swords of the Saracen; it's a certainty that Charles is among them—I dream of his touch as I sleep beneath the burning sand.

I sift the bones of the dead abandoned in the wastes; I do not find Charles, but I do uncover weaponry and treasures that I use to pay his debts in Haifa.

A Memory contains up to three Experiences. Each Memory should be defined by a theme, trait, or other subject that links its component Experiences in an intelligible way. Whenever a new Experience doesn't fit into an existing Memory, place it in a new Memory—assuming one is available.

Your vampire is allowed five Memories. Older Memories are lost when new Experiences occur and you have no place to put them. If you have filled all five Memories and need to start a new one, strike out an existing Memory and all of the Experiences it contains—forgetting things is a fundamental aspect of the game so embrace it.

The decision about which Memories are lost belongs to you as the player. It is not a decision that the Vampire is consciously making. Unless instructed otherwise, you may strike out any Memory you like to make room for a new Experience.

There is one way to preserve Memories when you run out of space. Instead of losing an existing Memory, you can move it into a **Diary**.

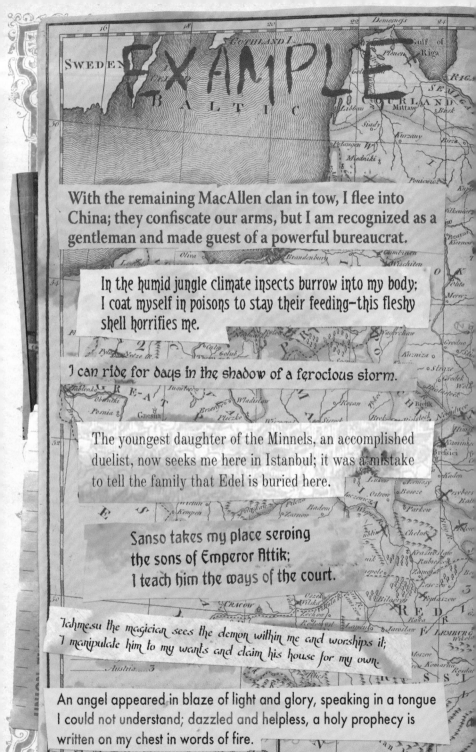

EXAMPLE

With the remaining MacAllen clan in tow, I flee into China; they confiscate our arms, but I am recognized as a gentleman and made guest of a powerful bureaucrat.

In the humid jungle climate insects burrow into my body: I coat myself in poisons to stay their feeding—this fleshy shell horrifies me.

I can ride for days in the shadow of a ferocious storm.

The youngest daughter of the Minnels, an accomplished duelist, now seeks me here in Istanbul; it was a mistake to tell the family that Edel is buried here.

Sanso takes my place serving the sons of Emperor Attik; I teach him the ways of the court.

Tahmesu the magician sees the demon within me and worships it; I manipulate him to my wants and claim his house for my own.

An angel appeared in blaze of light and glory, speaking in a tongue I could not understand; dazzled and helpless, a holy prophecy is written on my chest in words of fire.

EXPERIENCES

Russian nobles bribe me to cleanse undeeded lands of freeholders; I empty the peasants' minds and send them to work my stronghold in the East.

Callwyn and I construct an enclosed room in the back of our motorhome; at night he does not see the Moon and during the day I do not see the Sun.

I bed soldiers as a benediction; during the day they fight my battles and at night they feed my hungers.

I adopt the life of a wandering tinker and come to find joy in this simple trade; in the shadow of Bavarian Alps I am known by the name Hubertus and hailed as a jolly fellow.

THE NEWSPAPER REPORTERS DEMANDED SOMETHING FANTASTIC AND I GAVE IT TO THEM—THE MURDERER'S HEAD WOULD BE PRESERVED IN A JAR AT THE UNIVERSITY.

I can no longer easily tell humans apart, so my feeding taboos fall away with the years— all blood is wetness for my dried husk.

Diary

A Diary can hold up to four of your vampire's Memories. Unlike Memories themselves, Diaries are physical objects that are added to your Resource list. You may freely create a Diary whenever you need to move a Memory into it. Like any other Resource, a Diary can be lost. When this happens strike out the Memories it held. Your vampire can have one Diary at a time, and it must contain at least one Memory.

A Memory placed in the Diary is no longer in the vampire's head—it exists only in the Diary and the vampire accepts whatever is written as truth. Once a Memory has been transferred to a Diary, you may not add any further Experiences to that Memory.

To move a Memory to your Diary simply indicate that the Memory is now written in the Diary. For example, you might write "Diary" next to the Memory or connect it to the Diary icon on the character sheet with a drawn arrow.

When you create a Diary, give it a short description and add it to the Resource list. It might say something like:

Diary – a sturdy, leather-bound book

Diary – a collection of pictogram-adorned pots

Diary – gold filigree signs bordering a frightening ritual mask

Diary – a password-protected forum on an archaic website

Skills

Skills describe the capabilities and characteristics of your vampire. They indicate what your vampire **can do** and what they **might do**. *Swordplay, Relaxing Banter, Operate Heavy Machinery, I Do Not Blink The Sand Away*, and *I Teach the Nanissáanah* are all acceptable Skills. When instructed to record a new Skill you should relate it to the content of the Prompt.

What will it feel like for a vampire to use a Skill tied to a Memory that has been long lost?

Some Prompts will instruct you to **check** a Skill. To do this, place a checkmark next to that skill on your record sheet. Mechanically, this indicates that the Skill has been used. Narratively, a checked Skill gives you something to flavor your answers to later Prompts.

If unchecked Skills are what your vampire is capable of, checked Skills are what they have done. They are a part of your vampire's being—they are who the vampire is. Of course, it is entirely possible that your vampire might have Skills that you do not want to check. Instead of fighting this, revel in the plight of your humane vampire when they go to help a friend out of a bureaucratic jam and find that the only Skill they can check is *Rage and Kill*.

You may only check a Skill once. If you are instructed to lose a Skill, strike it out—it is gone and no longer influences the way your vampire moves through the world.

Resources

Resources are assets or structures that are useful to your vampire, or items that they value. *Knightly equipage, a loyal impi, a diamond tiara, the Castle Umbrecht, a business empire, a lucky penny, a screened-in charabanc, a Roman legion, the silvered key to the potentate's treasure vault, a carboy of acid, a box of tallow candles*—all are acceptable and engaging Resources.

In the Prompts there will occasionally be reference made to Stationary Resources. These are possessions that cannot be physically hauled away with the vampire when they leave the area. Examples might be *a haunted cave, an elephant-sized statue of Set, a chandlery, a hidden pit house, a hereditary title to land.*

When a Prompt instructs you to create Resources, be sure to create Resources that are contextually appropriate—even if this leads to Resources that aren't necessarily the most exciting or most useful. When a Prompt causes your

vampire to lose a Resource, strike it out. Leave the entry legible because lost things might come back in time.

Let your available Resources flavor how you write your Experiences. Curry your horse, ply your whip, command your submarine. Let Resources figure prominently when you are made to strike them out; don't just lose your mansion but burn it to the ground, or at least describe a fierce legal battle over the deed.

Don't limit your vampire's stuff to the Resources listed on the record sheet when answering Prompts—of course your rich Flemish vampire will have a fencing foil if one is needed, it's just not a Resource which can be spent to satisfy the mechanical needs of the game. If tools or homes or tombs are needed for narrative color you may create them as needed, just don't write them down.

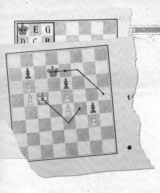

Characters

Characters are the people with whom your vampire has a relationship. Each Character should be named and described in a sentence fragment, such as *Lawrence Hollmueller, descendant of Baron Hollmueller* or *Sister Adelpho, a meddlesome nun*. Add more descriptors each time you interact with them in the course of resolving a Prompt. Lawrence, from the previous example, might become *Lawrence Hollmueller, descendant of Baron Hollmueller; I freed him from a Turkish prison*.

If it makes sense to include a Character when resolving a Prompt, do so even if the Prompt doesn't tell you to include a Character. In addition, create a new Character if a Prompt instructs you to include one but none are available.

A Character can be **mortal** or **immortal**; you will be told which type when you are instructed to create a new Character. Mortals are regular human beings or other creatures that die with the passage of time. Immortals, on the other hand, are supernatural beings for whom time has little meaning. They might be other vampires, angels or demons, ghosts, scientific experiments gone wrong, forgotten deities, underground lurkers, meddlesome ancestors, invisible shamblers, softly-spoken animated corpses, household gods or sprites, disembodied heads enduring cursed existences under bell jars, or anything else suitably bizarre.

Occasionally, you will realize that a Mortal must have died of old age. This might happen every four or five Prompts. When it does, strike out the Character's name. Outside of this, Characters cannot be killed unless a Prompt tells you to do so, but you can otherwise narrate about them as you would like.

Marks

A **Mark** is a visible indication of your vampire's undying state, or any other thing that sets them apart from mortal people. An ever-bleeding wound on the throat, eyes that are blank and white, a trailing specter, a ferocious scar, a hollow abdomen full of rats. A Mark is something your vampire carries for their entire existence.

When creating a Mark, consider whether your vampire conceals it, and how.

Example Marks include:

> A pair of great bat wings—
> I cut them off with a saw but the stubs remain;
>
> My eyes are hypnotic so I must we[ar] smoked glasses,
>
> A dark halo I cover with tall military hats;
>
> Under the Moon my shadow take[s] the shape of a jaguar;
>
> Animals fear me, children cry;
>
> I can become a wolf or a rat;
>
> I have hands with the fingers bent into backwards claws, I wear long sleeves to cover them from view.

WHAT IS A VAMPIRE?

The vampire is the character y[ou] will follow through the narrativ[e.] How they manifest their vampir[-] ic nature is up to you, but *Thou[-] sand Year Old Vampire* make[s] several assumptions. To get th[e] best experience out of this gam[e] system, your vampire…

> …should prey on human being[s] for sustenance;
>
> …should seek to camouflage them[selves] among those on which they feed;
>
> …should have been a human once, and still have human needs in one sense or another;
>
> …should be susceptible to environmental dangers that regular mortals might not care about, such as sunlight;
>
> …should be practically immortal;
>
> …should be mostly a loner.

The Prompts in Thousand Year Old Vampire are not necessarily geared toward complex political machinations between factions of immortal beings.

Vampire Creation

Start by imagining a person in the distant past—a Roman emperor, a Mesopotamian midwife, a French knight. This person will become your vampire. Imagine when and where they were born and who they were in life. Start a Memory with one Experience that encapsulates their history. For instance: *I am Henri, son of Jon, born near the Loire Valley in the 13th Century of Our Lord; I am a poor knight swindled out of my inheritance.*

This first Experience is a little different than most Experiences in that it's a broad summary of the vampire's life before becoming an undead thing. This Experience will be slotted into the character record's first Memory.

Next, create at least three Mortals and add them to the vampire's record sheet. These Mortals will have a relationship with your vampire—relatives, friends and lovers, enemies, mentors, debtors, or anything else appropriate for the time and place you have chosen. Describe each Character in a few words. Know that these Characters can and should be very important, but will not be around for long.

Give your vampire-to-be three Skills fitting for their lot in life, and three Resources they obtained while still mortal. Remember, Resources can be almost anything. Big or small, a Resource is a Resource whether it's an obsidian knife or a fleet of war ships.

Then, create three more Experiences—with one Experience each being entered into a separate Memory. Each of these Experiences should combine two of your vampire's traits. If your vampire has *the Longship* Bøkesuden as a Resource and the Character *Gundar, a Viking jarl, like a father to me,* you might write an Experience like *Gundar takes me on my first voyage aboard the Longship* Bøkesuden; *his touch calms me when we first leave sight of land.*

Lastly, create an Immortal. This is the creature that gifted (or cursed) your vampire with unlife. Create a Mark and an Experience that explain how your vampire became a creature of the night. One such Immortal is *Baron Hollmueller, an Austrian noble and a vampire; he stole the deed to my land*. The corresponding Experience might be *I duel the eerie Baron Hollmueller across the roof of the* *abbey; he nearly cuts my head from my shoulders but I do not die*, which leads to the Mark *My neck is permanently broken, I wear tight scarves and walk slowly to maintain my dignity*.

Once you have finished with your vampire, they will have three Skills, three Resources, a Mark, at least three Mortals, one Immortal, and one Experience in each of their five Memories.

Playing the Game

To play *Thousand Year Old Vampire*, you answer a series of Prompts. Answer these Prompts to learn about your vampire, experience their travails, and be surprised by their doings. Responding to the Prompts in satisfying ways is the joy of this game. After you've played through a few times you can find additional Prompts in Appendix I.

You can answer Prompts either in writing, like a journal, or just aloud to yourself. This book is designed so that you can write your responses directly onto its pages, if you are brave. Number your entries to keep the chronology straight.

In the process of answering Prompts, you create, lose, and alter your vampire's traits as instructed. **Every time** you answer a Prompt you must create an Experience and add it to a Memory unless instructed otherwise.

Roll your d10 and d6, and subtract the result of the d6 from that of the d10. If the result is a positive number, move forward that many Prompts; if it is a negative number, move backwards instead. A 0 means you encounter the same Prompt a second time.

Let us imagine that I have just answered Prompt 11. I roll 7 on the d10 and 4 on the d6, which means that I move forward three and end up at Prompt 14. However, if I rolled 4 on both dice, I would answer Prompt 11 again.

You will notice that Prompts have second and third entries. These are encountered the second and third times you land on a Prompt. If you land on a Prompt and have already responded to all the entries, move along to the next Prompt.

If you are instructed to check a Skill but have no unchecked Skills available, lose a Resource instead. Likewise, if you cannot lose a Resource when instructed to do so, check a Skill. When either of these substitutions occur it indicates that things have gone very badly for your vampire—narrate the worst possible outcome. Only Skills and Resources may be substituted for each other. You may not choose to lose Characters, Memories, or Marks in place of a Skill or Resource.

If you must lose a Skill or Resource and you have none, then your game is over— narrate your vampire's demise using the Prompt for inspiration.

The Game Ends...

...if you are unable to check or lose a Skill or Resource when required to do so, or if a Prompt tells you that the game has ended.

Two Styles of Play

There are two ways to play *Thousand Year Old Vampire*: As a **Quick Game** or a **Journaling** Game.

In a Quick Game, answer the Prompts entirely in the Memory area of your character record. This method is fast and satisfying, and gives you greater flexibility in interpreting your vampire's story.

In the Journaling Game, you keep a diary. Answer the Prompts in writing, dedicating a short paragraph or so to each question. You will end up with a document that you can look back at later. In addition to a journal entry, you must still add an Experience for each Prompt.

In the case of any contradictions or complications, your Memories and Experiences take precedence over the detail of your journal entries in the Journaling Game. As you play, you will come to understand aspects of the story that may not have been clear earlier on. You can modify or ignore earlier journal entries if needed, but you may never modify Memories unless instructed to do so by a Prompt!

Answering Prompts

Answer Prompts in a way that feels natural. Never force things. If relationships between existing Traits or past events relate to a Prompt, work them in. You do not need to answer every question in the Prompt.

Prompts will often combine to tell stories. If a helpful Character was introduced in one Prompt and the following Prompt has the vampire acquire a new Resource, find the relationship between them. Any amount of time can pass between Prompts, so several Prompts might join together to make a story arc that lasts days or decades.

Cede control to the game. Prompts are sparks for creativity and connection. Feel free to gently reinterpret answers to earlier Prompts to better make sense of current situations. But you should not try to tie everything together, it's not necessary. Your vampire will live for a thousand years, and many small, unresolved events will occur during their existence. Sometimes a Character will appear and then leave the game without accomplishing anything of note, or a Resource will go unused, both of which are fine— that's just how life, or un-life, is.

Be Innocent.

The Inquest Is in Progress—Priest Probably Will Be Discharged.

Lorain, Ohio, May 5.—For the first time since the tragedy, Casimir Reichlin, the younger brother of the murdered girl, who was in the house last Thursday night when the crime was committed, has told

Overthinking is unhelpful.
Not every Prompt needs to be important. You do not need to explain every decision you make while answering a Prompt. You can let some of it wait until later. Let the game bring back what matters.

Be uncomfortable.
Your protagonist is a vampire, even if you try to keep them decent and humane. Terrible and delicious things are going to happen. You should have moments of discomfort as Prompts combine with constrained resources to result in your vampire murdering loved ones and performing strange deeds. This is a strength of the game, so let darkness fall where it may.

Prompts are opportunities to learn about history and the real world. Turn to Wikipedia and read about the different types of Turkish nobility if you need to.

The game will wait.

The Passage of Time

This game is about the grind of centuries. Your vampire will lose their very memories to the passage of years and must pursue continuous reinvention to keep up with the evolution of society around them. Time is very loose, so imagine its progression as you like. Think about historical events and work them in when it feels right; world wars and political upheavals are hugely important events, even for vampires.

For general guidance, consider the first seven or eight Prompts you answer to be the first busy years after your character becomes a vampire. Everyone they know is still alive and the world is still the world of their mortal life. By contrast, their final Experiences might take place in the early 21st century.

Don't fret about specific years, but do watch for obvious breaks in the timeline. A series of Prompts might interrelate to tell a small story, only for something to interrupt that story. Take the opportunity to jump a few decades ahead. However, if you reach a game-ending Prompt and it's only the Fifteenth Century, that's fine too.

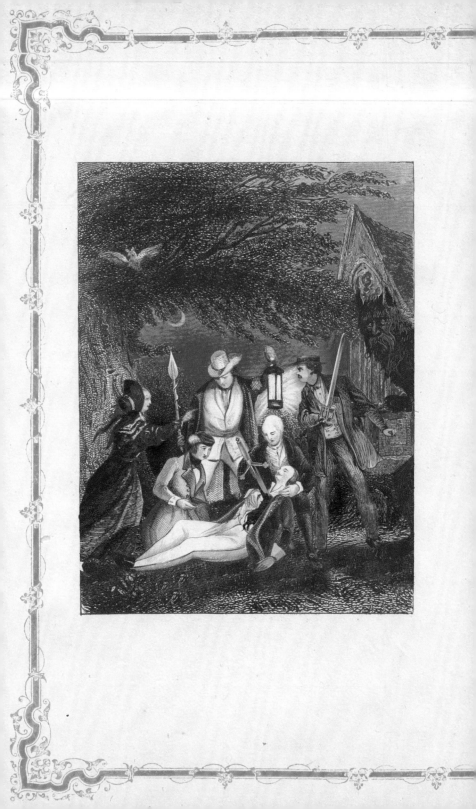

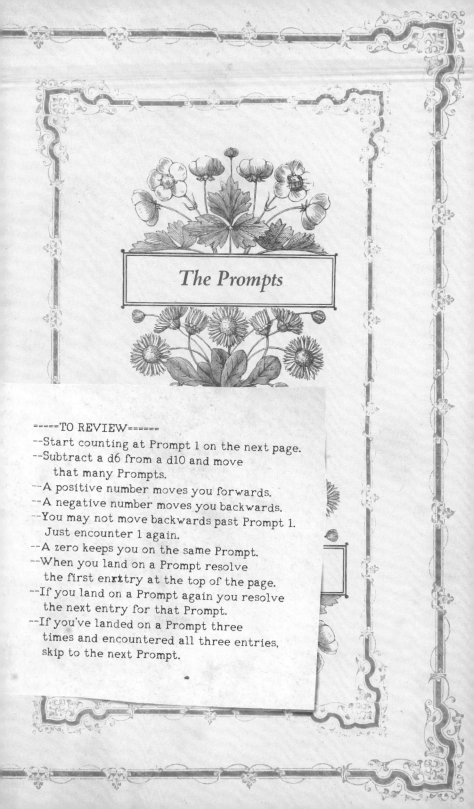

The Prompts

=====TO REVIEW======
--Start counting at Prompt 1 on the next page.
--Subtract a d6 from a d10 and move
   that many Prompts.
--A positive number moves you forwards.
--A negative number moves you backwards.
--You may not move backwards past Prompt 1.
   Just encounter 1 again.
--A zero keeps you on the same Prompt.
--When you land on a Prompt resolve
   the first enrttry at the top of the page.
--If you land on a Prompt again you resolve
   the next entry for that Prompt.
--If you've landed on a Prompt three
   times and encountered all three entries,
   skip to the next Prompt.

1 In your blood-hunger you destroy someone close to you. Kill a mortal Character. Create a mortal if none are available. Take the skill *Bloodthirsty.*

You are overcome by panic and maul someone close to you, accidentally turning them into a monster like yourself. Convert a beloved mortal Character into an enemy immortal. Take the Skill *Ashamed.*

You are captured and enslaved by a wicked and powerful supernatural entity. Create an immortal Character. How do you eventually escape their servitude? Check a Skill and take the Skill *Humans are Cattle.* Strike out all mortal Characters, as a hundred years have passed. Take a Resource you have used for evil while in service to your former master.

2 Horrified at your new nature, you withdraw from society. Where do you hide? How do you feed? Create a stationary Resource which shelters you.

You reinvent your existence around the seclusion of your hiding place. You begin to work in an artful way, changing your living environment. How do you come to appreciate beauty or craft in a new way? Create a Skill based on a Memory.

Your hiding place is destroyed by mortals. What steps had you taken to ensure your survival? What revenge do you wreak upon your persecutors? Degrade a Resource into ruins. Take the Skill *Vile Acts*.

3

A loved one discovers your condition and works to help you. Create a Resource which represents their assistance. Create a mortal Character if none are available.

You manipulate this mortal into committing atrocious deeds on your behalf. What do you do when they quail at these awful tasks? Take the Skill *Humans are Tools*.

At the end of the mortal's life you convert them into a mindless meat machine, an undying thing from which you feed. What regrets do you have? Change the Character to a Resource. Check a Skill.

4 You are exposed and flee to a neighboring region. Lose any stationary Resources. Check a Skill. A mortal flees with you. What new name do you adopt among these strangers?

You are adopted into a strange cult who take you in despite (or because of) your outlander origin. Check a Skill and create a Resource, *The Secret Cabal.* How did they find you? What vile initiation ceremony do you undergo? Do they know what you are?

The Secret Cabal, without your knowledge, performs a dark ceremony that changes a mortal Character into a horrific, alien and immortal thing. Convert a mortal Character into an immortal enemy. What alien objectives does this new immortal pursue? Did the Cabal manipulate you into helping with this creation? How does this change your relationship to the Cabal?

5

You murder someone you love or respect rather than let them expose you. Kill a Character. Check a Skill. If you have no living Characters, kill no one and create a beloved mortal Character who you have betrayed.

A Character you've victimized comes to you in a dream. Do they curse or forgive you? Receive a Mark.

Love hidden within your soul propels you on a foolish quest for absolution from some great guilt. What wrong did you try to right? How do you fail and make everything much, much worse? Lose a Resource. Check a Skill.

6

A mortal Character begins serving you. Who are they? Why are they drawn to you? Create a new mortal Character.

A trusted mortal Character betrays you in a surprising way. Lose a Resource. Why did they do this? Why do you forgive them?

A mortal Character sacrifices themselves to save you. Check a Skill. Gain a Skill relevant to love or trust.

7

Your body manifests some trait related to the vampire that created you. How do you become more like them? Create a Skill that reflects this.

People see a horror in you that you cannot perceive in yourself. What Mark do you possess that you do not know about? Create a Mark and a suspicious mortal who has seen it. What name do the people call you when your back is turned?

Through grim work with iron and fire you remove a Mark. Record an Experience of pain and blood. Who do you blame? You may remove a Mark or replace an existing Mark with something worse.

8 You are recognized for what you are by another creature like yourself. Create an immortal Character, lose a Resource and gain a Skill. What did you lose to them?

You gain an advantage over an immortal Character. What do you take from them? What do you learn? Convert a Memory to a Skill; strike out that Memory. Gain a mysterious Resource.

A Character you've angered has powerful allies. Create a new enemy immortal Character who is the face of this mysterious group which harries you. Check a Skill to escape their grasp. Take the Skill *Time to Leave*. Move to a far-off region and lose any stationary Resources. Take a new name.

9 You develop a system for feeding. What is it? What happens to those who die? Create a Skill that reflects this.

You not only drink their blood but financially profit from your victims as well! How do you arrange this? What atrocity do you commit to protect this system? Check a Skill, create a Resource.

Another Character usurps your feeding system and improves it. Do you crawl back to your ouster, begging to be let back in? If so, then gain the Skill *Belly on the Ground*. If you instead build a new feeding system from scratch, check two Skills and gain one Resource.

10

The stars pinwheel above you in the night. The seasons are a blur. You are as an automaton, unconscious of the passage of decades. A century passes. Strike out a Memory. Strike out all mortal Characters.

A potent artifact, religious or magical or technological, falls into your hands. With it you can remake the world. What is this thing? Who seeks it? Create a mortal Character. Add the item as a Resource. If you still have it when you achieve any game ending result, you may rewrite the ending as you like. You must lose this item first if you lose Resources in an encounter with an immortal Character.

While fiddling with the artifact you accidentally bring about the end times. Devils rise, angels fall, spirits are made manifest. Human populations are levied in a war which will last centuries and decide the fate of the cosmos itself. Create a Character or Resource that represents the manifestation of a supernatural conflict that fits your story up to this point. Create two immortal Characters aligned with either side of the conflict who are now interested in your Vampire.

11

How do you find solace from the raging hunger within you? You may *lose* one checked or unchecked Skill.

You discover an internal focus which lets you maintain control of your vampire self. Lose a violent Memory and take the Skill *I Control the Beast* and rewrite any unchecked Skill as something new. What new name do you take to distance yourself from what you once were? How is the name symbolic?

Your control breaks. You slaver and kill and revel in blood. You are your hunger. What were the last words of your closest friendly Character, mortal or immortal, as you feasted upon them? Change a beloved Memory to a lie in which you murder to protect yourself. Create a Skill that invokes the name of a dead Character in a mocking way.

12

New laws or social mores make it harder for you to hide among the populace. How are you nearly caught and destroyed? Check a Skill. Create a Skill. Create a mortal criminal who assists you.

Working across generations you change the laws of society to your advantage. How do you bend leaders to your will? What do you change? Create a Resource.

A mortal protégé outstrips you. They are smarter, crueler, and more capable than you can ever be. They lock you in a dungeon—for what purpose do they use you? Create a wicked mortal Character.

13

Generations of the same family serve you. This line starts from any living mortal Character, or from the descendants of a dead mortal Character. What bizarre rituals do they tie to their servitude? Lose a Resource and create a *Servitors of the Lineage* Resource.

Your servants are numerous, enthusiastic, and sometimes useless. Create a Skill based on a Memory, this is the Skill you use to control them.

Your servants bring you a gift you do not want. Create a problematic Resource.

14

An enemy Character uses a lost Resource to turn your few friends against you. Check three Skills to regain the Resource, or check one Skill to barely survive. Which former friend did you kill? Where do you flee?

You were born in a time and place much different than that in which you find yourself now. What values must you set aside to survive in this strange world? Create an appropriate contemporary Skill based on your most recent Memory. What new name have you recently adopted?

How do you rise to a position of leadership in this place? What neighbors or populations do you subjugate through war and violence? Gain a Resource you took from someone who wanted nothing but peace.

15 While traveling you come into conflict with another immortal. Gain a Mark. Who are they? What trick did you play upon them? Create a new immortal Character.

An immortal proves to be much more than they appear. Check a Skill or else lose a Resource or Memory. Gain a Resource or Skill.

How does human society change drastically due to the meddling of immortals like yourself? Who benefits? What Resource do you lose? Gain one Resource, Skill or Mark.

16

Some mortals have banded together to hunt you, well-armed and wise to your tricks. How do you defeat or evade them? Create a mortal hunter related to one of your checked Skills. Check a Skill.

The hunters are persistent, capable, and well-informed. They know things about you that you don't—create a Mark that is revealed in a confrontation. You are driven into hiding in an unpeopled wasteland. Lose any stationary Resources. Learn a new Skill related to this desolate region. What new name comes to you in loneliness?

Returning to civilization you wreak a terrible vengeance upon the hapless descendants of your harassers. Songs will be sung of their suffering for a thousand years. Historians will use it as a benchmark for evil. Create a mortal Character that was innocent and good until you exacted your toll. Do not actually write down what acts you committed against these people.

17 You commit a despicable murder, but not for the sake of feeding. Why? Check a Skill. Remove a mortal Character, if you like.

You are hounded for your crime. Check a Skill, lose a Resource. Confess your crime to any Character. Convert an enemy to a friend or a friend to an enemy. If you must create a Character, you become lovers.

You fight a duel with a beloved Character, create one if you have none. Check a violent Skill or appropriate Resource and win by killing them, or gain a Mark and flee to another land.

Μόνη σιγη μεταμελ.σκεν ώς φέρει

18 You have fed too long in one place, destroying a community or social group. Who were they? How did the last community member die? Gain a scavenged Resource, lose a Resource.

A community outcast has survived and vows to revenge themselves upon you. How did you know them? How did they know to catch you at your most vulnerable? Create a mortal Character bent on your destruction.

You are hounded out of the land. Lose any stationary Resources. Check one Skill to escape, two to destroy your persecutor, three to make amends.

19

Two friendly Characters become embroiled in an internecine conflict. Become involved and check a Skill. Create up to two Characters, if needed. How do you profit? Gain a Resource.

You scheme while your friends make war on one another. Manipulate the conflict to destroy any Character.

Too much fighting, too much blood. Acting as peacemaker you try to end the conflict between former friends, but they both turn on you. Lose a Resource. Gain a Mark.

20 There is a great shift in the way society moves goods. How does this work to your advantage? Check a Skill. Create a Skill based on a Memory.

Your vampiric state enables you to manipulate people across generations, using them to your own advantage. Create one stationary Resource and one ostentatious Resource that symbolizes wealth and power.

Living off investments and rents makes you lazy and blunts your hunting edge. Check a Skill that is cruel or grasping, *lose* a checked Skill related to creativity or effort. Gain a stationary Resource that you didn't truly earn.

21 You are trapped outside when the sun rises and take shelter some place you are not supposed to be. A child discovers and befriends you. Create a mortal child Character and record a humanizing Experience.

The child teaches you to appreciate the world again. You see small things, you smile. Create a Skill based on a pleasant Memory.

Decades pass. The child has died of old age. You stand at their grave. What more could you have done to make their life better? How did you betray them? Strike out that Character with great ceremony.

22 Create a mortal Character. You have shaped them from infancy to be exactly what you want. Lose a Resource.

Your Diary is lost or stolen. Lose the Diary and all Memories it contains. If you have no Diary, lose one Resource. Create a Character who you wrongly blame for this loss.

You become a loner embedded in the now, manipulating a hundred threads to stay fed and safe. Lose a Memory slot permanently. Take the Skill *Feral Cunning*.

23

You master a strange new science or field of knowledge. How does your vampire nature give you special insight into these studies? Create an appropriate Skill based on a Memory.

You strike up a long correspondence and fall in love. Create a mortal Character. Go to them by giving up a Resource, or smother the love and lose a Memory.

Your mortal love dies through the machinations of another Character unless you check one Skill. If you do save them they will instead die of sickness, or accident, or old age. Either way, you keep a token by which to remember them. Create a Resource.

24

You are forced to adopt a new name. Why?

Erase the first sentence of any two Memories. You're not quite sure why. Do not create an Experience about this.

One place is as another to you, and you simply stop returning home. Lose a stationary Resource. Where do you wander?

25

Your methods for acquiring victims are no longer effective. What has changed? Lose a Resource and create a Skill which describes your new feeding techniques.

What physical labors are necessary to utilize this method? Create a simple, practical Skill and strike out a Memory.

A mortal Character discovers your feeding system. What compelling argument do they use to get you to abandon it? Check a Skill.

26

You accidentally create a vampire through sloppy feeding. Create an immortal Character from an existing mortal Character. Why do you not destroy them? Check a Skill.

This immortal Character lurks on the fringes of your existence. They become an embodiment of one of your least savory checked Skills. How do they act when your paths cross? What disturbing gift do they give you? Create a Resource.

This immortal Character falls into the hands of mortals, indirectly imperiling your existence. Save them by checking three Skills. Lose three Resources if you do not save them. If you cannot lose all three Resources, lose as many as possible and flee to a new land—from now on all humans know vampires are real.

27

Wars rage throughout the region in which you reside. You withdraw into a hidden retreat, waiting for them to pass. Lose a Resource.

Your secretive ways result in you being arrested as a spy. Check a Skill to escape or lose a Resource and gain a Mark from the experiments performed upon you. Either way, create a mortal who heads a well-funded organization that imperils creatures such as yourself.

You become a spy, selling out the land you call home. Gain two Resources. Check a Skill, gain a Skill, *uncheck* an ancient and surprising Skill. Which Character suffers and dies because of your actions?

28 A long dead mortal Character returns. What do they want from you? How have they survived death? You only recognize them if you still have a related Memory. Check a Skill.

What peril do they pull down upon you? Create a new enemy Character, mortal or immortal. Check a Skill or lose a Resource.

You are ceaselessly hunted by potent, supernatural beings. Describe the methods you develop to avoid detection. Lose a Memory to gain a Skill or Resource, or do not lose a Memory and create a mortal servitor.

29

You are exposed as a monster and flee to a far-off land. Lose any stationary Resources. You do not know the language of this new place—how do you overcome this obstacle? What new name do you take?

You disguise yourself with an entirely new persona. Take an old Memory and modify it to make it contemporary and bland. Create a Skill based on blending in.

You lose yourself in your assumed personality. Lose your oldest and newest Memories. Throw away your Diary. Create a Skill and Resource tied to your new life.

30 What social mores have your forgotten? Lose a checked Skill.

You feel a love forbidden by the convention of mortals around you. Create a new Character. Lose a Resource.

You reinvent yourself and how you relate to the world. Uncheck a Skill.

31

You fall into a deep slumber for a hundred years. Strike out any mortal Characters.

You recognize the descendant of a dead mortal who features in one of your Memories, and feel compelled to make their acquaintance. How do you share knowledge about their ancestor without revealing your monstrous nature? How is this conversation awkward? Gain a contemporary and unexpected Skill. Create a mortal Character, a new friend.

Your mortal friend discovers family documents that reveal you for what you are. How does your relationship change? You may regain a forgotten Memory related to the mortal's ancestor.

32

You keep a prisoner. Why this particular person? Why don't you feed upon them? Create a Character and a Skill related to keeping them captive.

Mortals rescue your prisoner. Create two mortal rescuers. Lose a Resource.

Your prisoner returns to you, but on their own terms. What is this strange new relationship?

33

You know where the old things are. Create a Resource and make an enemy Character into a friend.

You publish a book or in some other way cement a Memory (either current or from your Diary) in such a way that it can never be lost. Draw a star next to the Memory to indicate this and change the Memory to make it slightly less interesting. This Memory can never again be changed or struck out. It no longer takes up a Memory slot.

A massive shift of power happens in the mortal realm—governments fall, wars are waged, a new order is created. Who benefits? Check a Skill. Commit atrocious deeds to gain a Resource related to controlling innocent people. Take the Skill *Join the Winning Side* or instead check two Skills.

You destroy something important to you in a purposeless rage. Lose a precious Memory or destroy a Resource.

Your frenzies terrify even yourself. Do you learn to control them or instead choose to embrace this horror? Kill a mortal Character, if there is one, or create a Mark if not.

Pull the very skin from your face in an attempt to expunge yourself of lingering humanity. Create a Mark. How do you cover your disfigurement going forward?

35 You encounter the descendant of an old foe and help them in some way. Why did you do this? Check a Skill. Create a mortal Character.

They repay your kindness by lashing out at those they perceive as your enemies. A Character is killed.

The mortal is in grave peril. Check a Skill or lose a Resource to save them, otherwise they die a terrible death.

36

The deceptions you practice fool even yourself. Combine any three Traits to fabricate an Experience that you believe to be true.

Punish someone because of this false Memory. You kill a or maim a Character. Check a Skill. Take the Skill *I Know What's Real.*

One of your real Memories turns out to be completely fabricated, a fever dream spun of cobwebs. Completely erase one Memory.

37

Things fall to dust. Lose a Resource for which you have no corresponding Memory. Do not create a new Experience for this Prompt, it simply happens as you stare in silence.

You are a creature with habits of unknown origin. Lose an unchecked Skill for which you have no corresponding Memory.

Your thoughts are calcifying, your habits are tyrants. You are nearly captured by an enemy who has been studying your patterns over many years. Break a Resource and remake it into something new and surprising.

38 Your whole being becomes centered in your senses and your hungers. Create a Skill that demonstrates your feral vampire nature and lose an existing Memory.

You move differently than humans and they unconsciously sense it. Create a Mark.

You can always find the frail, the weak, the vulnerable. Take the Skill *Cull the Herd*. Do not meet the eyes of the strong—they are not for you.

39

Age has damaged your Diary. Strike out three nouns from the Memories in your Diary, starting from the oldest entry. If you have no Diary, do this to the first three nouns in a Memory of middling age.

You make a new copy of your crumbling Diary. In your most recent Diary Memory, swap two verbs each for the other. If you have no Diary strike out three verbs in your most recent Memories.

Find a character record from an earlier play through of this game. Swap a Memory for one from that character sheet.

40

How do you conceal yourself while you sleep? What steps have you taken for protection? Check a Skill and create a Resource. Create a mortal servant Character, if you like.

You are approached by a supernatural Character unknown to you. They take you on a bizarre journey, then offer you spiritual solace in exchange for a terrible pledge. What do they demand? Will you accept? If you accept, gain a Skill.

The potent beings which populate the spaces beyond sight have been revealed to you and nothing will ever be the same again. Let this bizarre world heavily influence the rest of your game. Take the Skill *I See In-Between*.

41

Your body is distant from human concerns.
Lose a Memory slot. Erase your oldest extant name.

A social convention or taboo from some long-forgotten part of your existence is hardwired into your being. What is it? How does this hinder your movement in society? Create a Mark.

A ghost haunts you, though you do not know if it is real or a manifestation of madness. Bring back a long dead Character as a spirit.

42

What piece of contemporary technology can you not interact with due to your vampire nature? How did your first encounter with this technology almost get you destroyed? Check a Skill.

You make the acquaintance of a group of mortals who share an interest in some Resource you possess. Is it a club? Are these friends? Create three mortal Characters. Develop a Skill related to the Resource in question.

Decades pass. You remain ageless as your friends slowly curl and dry up; you must leave or be exposed as a monster. Stand outside in the darkness, watching them laugh as they tell stories of how they miss you.

43 You have archaic ways in spite of your focus on blending in. Create a Resource based on a checked Skill that reflects this.

Swap around the proper nouns between two Memories. Do not create an Experience about this.

Examining a Resource you possess sparks a forgotten Memory. That Resource once belonged to another Character, but you had forgotten this. Gain tremendous insight into your history by recalling this Memory. Write this forgotten Experience into your Memory or directly into a Diary. To be clear, you are creating a new "forgotten" Experience, not bringing back a Memory you struck out.

44 An immortal Character you've met returns to claim a debt. What is it? How have they changed? Do you pay willingly? If you have a Memory of this Character you lose two Resources, if not then lose three Resources and check a Skill.

What did they do to send you into the darkest despair? *Erase* your earliest Memory. You will never get it back. Gain a Skill.

You develop a plan and carry it through with ruthless efficiency, bringing death and destruction to an immortal Character. You may either reclaim a Resource they took, or destroy them. Check a Skill.

45

Your body is undergoing further corruption and change. When do you first notice these new changes? Create a Mark.

Your body is becoming more effective as it becomes less human. Create a Skill based on one of your Marks.

You find companionship in a group of mortals who are in some way outside society. Do they know what you are? Would they care? Create two friendly mortal Characters, each related to one of your Marks.

46

You are exposed and flee to a far-off land. Convert any stationary Resources to a new Resource representing portable cash or treasure. What name do you travel under? What profession do you claim when you come to rest?

You flee again, this time to a far-off enclave or colony. How do you use colonial rule to your benefit? Choose one Skill: *Occupier, Insurgent, Inconspicuous,* or *Gone Native* along with an appropriate new name.

Revolution! As a suspicious outlander you are imprisoned. Escape by checking two Skills or bribe your way free with two Resources. Spend an additional Resource to rescue any traveling companions.

47

The world has evolved in ways you can't comprehend, causing you to lose a good amount of wealth. What happened? Check a Skill. Create a Skill that will hopefully prevent this happening again. Lose a Resource.

You have helpless people put in your charge. Create a Skill that helps you exploit them. Derive it from a happy Memory.

You are impressed by the fighting spirit of one of your victims. What did they do? How do they remind you of your own earliest memories? Did they survive? Create a mortal Character.

48

You awaken covered in dust. Generations have passed. Your sleeping place has been sealed off. How do you escape? Lose a Resource. Strike out all mortal Characters.

A Mortal you thought dead is still alive, somehow. Remarkable! Bring back the most recently struck out mortal Character.

In your long dreaming you discover a path to lands beyond the real, a fantastic place of enormous terrors and great beauty. You may abandon this Earth and go where none may follow; leave behind all Characters, Marks, and Resources except a Silver Sword and return to Prompt 10. Proceed forward from there, an unMarked vampire in a realm of dreams. If you land on this Prompt a second time, you awaken and can never return. If you do not travel to this dream land you instead take the Resource *A Handwritten Book of Fantastic Dreams*.

49

What simple, practical skill proves invaluable in your strange existence? How did you learn it? Create a Skill.

How did you come to be in a place of common laborers? What previously checked Skill convinced them to accept you? What was that night of camaraderie like? Create a mortal Character. Check a Skill.

Your new friends become a source of food. Create a Resource that reflects this.

50 You are captured in a trap set for predatory mortals. What sort of criminal are you taken to be? How does this experience help you learn to better prey on mortals? Make a new Skill that sours the purity of a pleasant Memory.

You are almost uncovered and must dramatically shift your hunting patterns. Become a member of the lowest classes and lose a Resource. If you already are of the lowest classes instead become a member of the highest and check a Skill.

You take up with predatory mortals. Create a repugnant mortal Character who becomes your associate. Even you fear these people. Why?

51

When you hunger too much you become a hunting creature bereft of intellect. Lose a random Experience from a Memory somewhere in the middle of your Memory list.

You find companionship in something that is not human. Is it an animal, or maybe something inanimate? How do you interact with it? How did you find it, or did it find you? Create either a Character or Resource to represent this companion.

All things end, but apparently not this. A mortal Character for whom you hold great affection is un-aging. Is it magic? Some form of infection? They still count as a mortal Character, but they will never die of old age.

52 The beauty of the dawn calls you. Create an additional Memory slot dedicated to beauty, nature, or peace.

You stay long enough to hear the end of a morning bird's song. You are burned by the Sun—create a Mark.

Stretch out your arms, feel the warmth. The light pushes through your eyelids and you are not consumed in fire. Sunlight (or some other environmental condition) no longer harms you. Create a Skill about freedom.

53 A mortal Character you trusted, or one of their descendants, leads a hunting party. What shared secrets are being used against you? Check a Skill.

You have the troublemaking Character at your mercy. Record an Experience of forgiveness.

Mors certa hora incerta

They betray you again and escape. Lose a Resource or gain a disfiguring Mark.

54 Your strange accent and old ways always reveal you as an outsider, mocked and cheated at best or hated at worst. Smother these useless traits by converting an old Memory to a new Skill for blending in.

OMNIA

MEA

Your old memories are changing to reflect the attitudes you need in the present. Change a Memory to incorporate anachronistic, contemporary aspects. Do not create a new Experience.

Discard a Resource that is more than a hundred years old.

MECUM

PORTO

55

Timeless introspection becomes manifest in creative acts. Choose a creative Skill based on a lost Memory.

You dedicate yourself to an art. Lose a Resource but gain back one lost Memory.

You achieve fame for your art but must remain in shadow. Destroy a Resource in frustration. Gain a Skill.

To name the unknown misscellany poems

56

You begin a fantastic construction that puzzles the mortals around you. Give just a hint as to its purpose. Lose a Resource and gain the Skill *Visionary*.

Mortals try to prevent you from realizing your vision. Check a Skill to persevere. What awful crime did you commit to protect your construction?

You've finished your construction. Why did you make this? Does it have a function? Does it change the world?

57

Your knowledge of old things becomes a strength. Based on a checked Skill, what knowledge do you share with contemporary mortals? Check a Skill. Create a Resource.

What humans seek you out for your knowledge? What do you give them? What do you take? Create a mortal Character who is smarter and more capable than you. Gain a Resource.

You are brought to the site of one of your oldest crimes. Who brought you here? Why? Do you even remember? Check a Skill. If you have no Memory of this crime, you will be reminded.

58 Society has changed. How has travel become easier for you? Recover any stationary Resources for which you still have a Memory, they are re-added to your Resource list.

What memories are unearthed by wandering these old places? Get back a lost Memory related to the stationary Resource, or gain a new treasure Resource which you'd concealed here.

What grisly trap was set for you here? Lose a Resource, gain a Mark.

A mortal discovers the journals of a long dead Character, or your own lost Diary, and approaches you. What do they seek? Gain a Skill or a Resource. Create a mortal Character.

The mortal harms, shames or exposes you. Check a Skill as you fruitlessly pursue them. Lose a Resource.

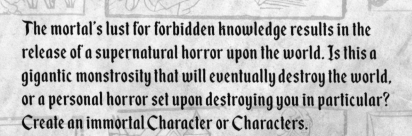

The mortal's lust for forbidden knowledge results in the release of a supernatural horror upon the world. Is this a gigantic monstrosity that will eventually destroy the world, or a personal horror set upon destroying you in particular? Create an immortal Character or Characters.

60 Check a Skill to avoid arrest as a criminal. What happened? Who was arrested in your place? Create a mortal Character if necessary.

Create an innocent mortal Character. They were executed for a crime you committed. What hobby were you tinkering with the night they were put to death? Take the Skill *It's None of my Concern.*

An entire class of people are blamed for crimes you committed. Take the Skill *Always Have a Scapegoat.* Who suffers in your place? Create a friendly Character who represents these people and is ignorant of your complicity. Create another Character who is in a position of authority: they know these people are innocent but do not care.

61 Someone reminds you of a beloved Character long dead. Check a Skill to curry their acquaintance. Create a mortal Character.

You frequently confuse living mortals with a dead Character. Take the Mark *I See [dead Character] Everywhere.*

Your body is ancient. A Mark becomes disabling. You must seek mortal assistance. Create a mortal Character who is especially capable of helping you.

62 You realize that some ancient taboo or limitation you long believed in no longer applies. What circumstances prompted this discovery? How does this make your existence more satisfying? Change one checked or unchecked Skill in a way that's relevant.

You discover a point of weakness where you were once strong. What have the ages taken from you? What causes this condition? Lose a checked Skill.

HORMAGAUNT

You receive an injury which incapacitates you. Left alone you would recover, but helpful people rush you to a hospital. There you awaken, and realize that you are known. Create a Character: a horrified mortal medical professional who knows exactly what you are.

63

How do you provide for your banal, material needs? Record an Experience about the time this went wrong. Check a Skill.

How do you avoid the eye of the government? Create a Skill based on a Memory.

How do you try to fool yourself into thinking you provide a valuable service to society? Take the skill *Parasite*.

64

Vast numbers of humans are migrating around the world. What group becomes easy to feed upon? How do you capitalize on their helplessness? Create a Resource.

You manipulate society's leaders to make one group of humans even more vulnerable to your vampiric feeding. What system do you build around victimizing these people? Check a Skill, create a relevant Skill from a Memory. Create a Character who is central to those resisting your machinations.

Society collapses on a global scale and will not recover for centuries. Millions starve, governments dissolve, there is murder in the streets as cities burn. How do you take advantage of the chaos? Check a Skill. Create two new Resources. Create a Skill. What Character rises to a position of global leadership in these awful times?

65

A possession turns out to have financial value as an antique. Trade your oldest Resource for two contemporary Resources.

You experience intense regret over a Resource you have given away or lost. Do anything to get it back. Lose two Resources or check two Skills and get back one lost Resource.

Objects are transient. All is nothing. Throw away your oldest or most precious Resource.

66

Your knowledge is outmoded. Lose an unchecked Skill which is now useless.

Your concept of value is outdated. Lose a Resource.

You are so ancient you no longer look like the people of today. Create a Mark that reflects this. How do you come to realize that your very body no longer fits in?

67

Language itself leaves you behind. People discuss concepts you cannot grasp using tools you cannot understand. How is this problem dramatically made manifest? Create a Character who will teach you a Skill to help you offset this disadvantage.

New forms of communication offer new ways to hunt. Modify an old Memory to include an anachronistic use of this sort of contemporary communication technology. Check a Skill, create a Skill.

Language has grown into something outside your ken. You can invoke phonemic patterns to which mortals will react in certain ways, but you can no longer share actual thoughts or feelings or abstract ideas. Create a Skill that expresses this.

68 An antiquity has surfaced which is directly tied to your mortal life. Check a Skill or lose a Resource and gain the antiquity as a Resource, then regain one of your earliest Memories. Record an Experience about acquiring the antique.

Because of this antiquity someone has begun to hunt you. Create a mortal Character. How do they almost expose you? Check a Skill or lose a Resource.

The mortal Character hunter corners you. You become the embodiment of one of your Checked Skills to defeat them. Take a Mark.

69

You bond with an ancient enemy Character over your shared past, finding in it something more comprehensible than this modern world. Check a Skill. You become friends. Share a Resource and gain a Resource that is shared with you.

You and your friend retire to a hidden place. There you share real pleasure for the first time in centuries. Create a Skill about love and safety.

You and your friend concoct a fantastic plan and bring it to fruition. Check a Skill. What is it? Do you conquer the world? Raise the dead? You may end the game now, if appropriate.

Mortals are cruel and work in ways outside your understanding. How were you mocked or victimized? Why was your response ineffectual and costly? Check a Skill.

An important Memory is tainted by your exposure to the psychological tricks of contemporary society. Modify a Memory to make it less special. Lose an unchecked anti-social Skill.

Lose a Memory. Record an Experience driven by a desire for contemporary prestige items. Lose two Resources, gain one prestigious Resource.

71

An immortal Character has been destroyed by mortals. How did you come to find out about this? What did you lose? Create a Skill based on a Memory. Create an immortal Character if necessary.

How were you unintentionally responsible for this killing? What minor benefit did you gain? Gain a Resource.

Create a false Experience about an immortal Character, which helps you make peace with your memories of them.

72

You are caught outside and destroyed. What happened? The game is over.

73

You achieve a position of absolute stability that might sustain you, unchanging, until the Sun dies.
What does this mean? The game is over.

74

You are physically trapped in a place from which you will never be rescued. What do you think about for the first thousand years? The game is over.

75

An old friend or foe murders you in your sleep.
What do you see in those seconds between dream
and non-existence? The game is over.

76

A government captures you, knowing you for what you are. What do they do with you? The game is over.

77

Your body finally wears out. You cannot carry out your feeding patterns. What happens? The game is over.

78

Creatures like yourself have taken over the Earth.
What is your position in this new world?
The game is over.

79

You discover a way to become mortal. Do you take it?
How will this go wrong? The game is over.

80

You translate yourself into a higher plane. What does this mean? The game is over.

Appendix I
Alternate Prompts

• To be enjoyed in place of regular Prompts •
• Save your original Prompt page and use one of these in place of that number •
• Not all of these have multiple entries! •
• These aren't in any particular chronological order, proceed with caution •
• Some of these might be odd, or repetitive, or nonsensical •
• Some might break the rules or be unclear, just roll with it •

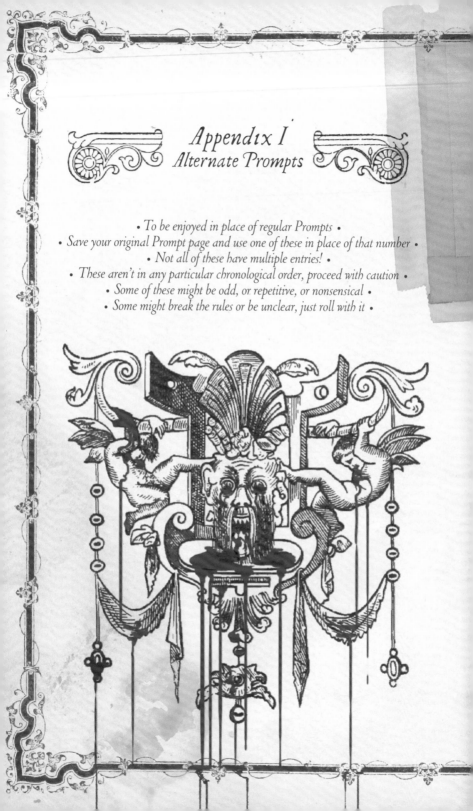

1. You are compelled to make a vow that is nearly impossible to keep. Why are you being made to do this? What penalty will you pay for breaking your word? Create a Resource *The Vow I Keep*.

2. As you feed on mortals, another being is feeding on creatures like you. However, it is not unkind. Create an immortal Character who both menaces and helps.

3. Your tastes become rarefied, your needs extreme. What further stipulations are placed on your feeding?

4. What night of the year is significant to you? How do you mark it?

5. What vermin haunt your sleeping place? Do these provide any useful service or are they just a nuisance?

   What do the vermin feed upon in your sanctuary? What things feed on them in turn? Create a Resource that is somehow related to this.

   The tiny dramas played out by these creatures come to fascinate you. You give them names and involve yourself in their stories. Choose one of your fiercest subjects, give it some appropriate Traits, and run it through the Prompt Chart starting with the first entry. Modify the Prompts as necessary to fit into this tiny, grave world. Continue this until you tire of it. Claim for yourself one of the Skills the creature learned. If appropriate, add the creature as a Character.

6. What disease have you begun to spread to those you bite? Gain a Mark. What Characters have you infected?

   People begin to investigate the strange spread of this disease. Who is it? Scientists? Government representatives? Vampire hunters? Wherever you go this plague begins to blossom. Check a Skill. Create two mortal Characters with divergent interests in this mysterious affliction.

   Those you've infected with your disease become something... else. What are they? This has far-reaching effects as carriers spread across the globe, infecting others. The geopolitical landscape itself is permanently altered. Lose a Resource to these changing times. Gain a Skill which helps you thrive in this new world. Create a mortal who rises to prominence.

7. At what contest does a mortal best you? What boon must you grant? Check a Skill or lose a Resource as appropriate. Create a mortal Character.

8. A temple or monument is dedicated to some mortal you knew long ago. How do you react when you learn of this? Is it appropriate? If you still remember the mortal gain one Resource. If you possess something that belonged to the mortal you may trade it for two Resources.

9. Something once only possible for a vampire is now done better by modern technology. What is it? How does this affect you? Check a Skill.

10. You spend decades haunting a piece of architecture, lurking in the shadows throughout the night. What draws you here? Check a Skill. Create a Skill tied to this place.

11. You live in a marginal place, a non-space between other things. It's a gap between the defined worlds that make up society, yet is somehow its own microcosm proof against the rule of authority. How does this space mirror the larger world outside? Who else congregates here and why? Create a Skill about being parallel to, but outside of, the strictures of culture. Create two different Characters who are here for very different reasons.

12. You begin to burrow. What drives you to shift the earth, sliding ever downwards toward the core the planet? Create a Skill.

   You meet another haunter of the dark, a ghoul who feeds on rotting corpse flesh. They are wary but not unfriendly. What marvels do they show you in their underground world? What secrets do you learn? Create an immortal ghoul Character.

   Here among the glowing grave slabs and miasmic corpse pits you find someone you thought long dead. They've abandoned their humanity and are a necrophagous ghoul-thing like they who brought you here. You are told a story which involves two other Characters you once knew. This lost Character gifts you with either an arcane and mysterious Resource or with a revelation about your own past (represented by a Skill). Will you stay here forever or return to the surface? Will this rediscovered Character join you? This may be an appropriate time to end the game.

13.   How did you come to be a guest of these rich and powerful people?
      Check a Skill. Gain a related Skill. Create two thoughtlessly wealthy
      mortal Characters.

      You enchant your hosts. They do not share their wealth, but simply
      being around them confers indirect benefits. Create a Resource or Skill
      that reflects this.

      These people tire of you. You are no longer invited into their
      homes, are unwelcome at their gatherings. You discover you've
      incurred significant financial debts of which you were not aware.
      Lose two Resources and check a Skill. Create a Character whose job
      it is to enforce the will of the rich and powerful.

14.   You've learned more about human anatomy and physiology than any
      mortal could learn in a single lifetime. At least not without murdering
      the living as you do. Gain an appropriate Skill.

      You fall in with a medical crowd; doctors, students, graverobbers,
      anatomists. You turn your darkly won knowledge to profit. Create
      a Resource denoting a small amount of wealth. Create a Character
      of the medical profession who is drawn to you. They are a
      dangerous person.

      A Character of whom you are fond is seriously injured. You
      rush them to a medical friend for help and everything goes wrong.
      What did you do to cause this disaster? You are forced to flee
      the region and adopt a new name in a far-off place. Lose all
      stationary Resources.

15.   You confess your story to a mortal who writes it down. They do not
      believe you, but it makes for good fiction. Learn a Skill about tale
      telling. Create a mortal Character who is a writer.

      Your stories prove popular. The writer pays you with a small Resource
      and pressures you for more. You begin to fabricate new stories and in
      the doing confuse yourself about the truth. Take any two Experiences
      and merge them into one new memory which makes you seem heroic.

      You visit the writer. Terrified and pale, they push a manuscript at
      you. It's your true story, supported by irrefutable evidence. They
      know what you are. How do you stop them from publishing
      this book?

16. What superstitions have been created about you? How do you hear of them? Create a Skill that capitalizes on these fears.

> Some of the wards and weapons prove efficacious. Everyone is surprised, especially you. Check a Skill and lose a portable Resource.

> > These new vulnerabilities prove key to learning about your nature. In an ancient library you learn about things like yourself. Create an immortal Character like yourself who does not know you exist.

17. You come to need some sort of mechanical adjunct for your body to function properly. What is it? Create or modify an appropriate Mark.

18. You unconsciously take up a forgotten habit, gesture, or saying from your mortal days. It becomes a fad and you are the epitome of it. Create an appropriate Skill or Resource.

19. Sit quietly in the darkness, hear the creaks and drips. Close your eyes and rest this book in your lap. Wait for the sun to round the planet.

> Why are you still here? Go outside and explore the night. Feel where your mind is drawn as you walk in the darkness.

> > Bury this book somewhere in the dark. Dig it up the next night. This is good practice for other things.

20. A wrong you've long mulled you now forgive.

21. You push aside the empty superstitions of your past. These dead traditions have no merit. Create a Skill.

22. *Eventful times:* Generate three Prompts and resolve them all as one.

23. You are surprised that being in the presence of a particular expression of religious belief causes you discomfort. Create a Skill about recognizing and avoiding victims who might practice this tradition.

> Some very specific gesture or item within a religious tradition causes you debilitating pain and may even be capable of destroying you. Create a Mark that reflects this. Create a Character who somehow embodies this aspect of the religion. Avoid this person.

> > One religious tradition in particular proves to be irrefutably true. How does this affect your world view? How did you come to learn of the truth of this belief? Create a Skill.

24. You discover a technological principle or invention far before its time. How do you capitalize on this knowledge? Create a Resource.

> Over decades the technological breakthrough you made becomes common knowledge in your region. How does it change society? What advantage do you lose? Check a Skill.
>
>> Local leaders lever your discovery for conquest. Your region becomes the core of a continent spanning empire which will expand for centuries. Rage as you watch your hard work turned to the benefit of others. Lose one Resource.

25. A poet enraptures you with their art. You manipulate him and inadvertently crush their spirit, their poems are dead. Create a mortal Character devoid of purpose.

26. You become attached to a powerful, terrifying Character. As long as that Character is alive you gain Resources where you would lose them, but every Prompt must be described in terms of the Character's wickedness and your servility. A Character dies every Prompt you resolve, with the wicked Character dying last.

> This wicked character changes your body in a permanent, arbitrary way. Gain a Mark. Lose a Skill which you can no longer perform.

27. A peasant accuses you of being a vampire but is not believed. They are punished severely. Create a mortal Character.

> While traveling you come across the peasant begging for alms. For their accusations they've been put through ordeals that left them permanently harmed and exiled. They do not recognize you. Check a Skill.
>
>> You somehow deeply shame yourself: Either kill all living Characters or flee the region.

28. You meet a good-hearted traveler on a noble quest at a crossroads at midnight. After talking to them for a bit, you feed very well. Rob their corpse for a portable Resource.

> You are haunted by the last words of the traveler. What good deed had they failed to bring to completion? Create a Character whose suffering the traveler sought to relieve.
>
>> Complete the traveler's good deed. Check a Skill or lose a Resource. Your heart rests easier now; create a Skill which reflects this. How do you explain the traveler's death to the person you aided?

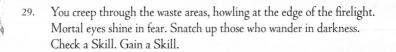

29. You creep through the waste areas, howling at the edge of the firelight. Mortal eyes shine in fear. Snatch up those who wander in darkness. Check a Skill. Gain a Skill.

30. A mortal child is born in a nearby community bearing one of your Marks. Create a mortal Character.

31. The Moon calls. Form a foolish plan to ascend to it. Lose a Resource in the attempt.

32. You meet a former victim socially. They recognize you. It is awkward, at the least. Create a mortal Character.

33. You are caught in the act of subduing a victim; a hue and cry is raised and you are cornered. You fear the worst but are instead lauded as a hero—the person you'd attacked was a terrible criminal. Create a Skill building on this positive reputation. Create a criminal Character bent on revenge.

34. The religious beliefs of your mortal years have become corrupted by contemporary people. Check a Skill then fail to put them on the proper path.

35. Locals have been coming to your sleeping place and using your recumbent body for oracular predictions. They honor you and leave small gifts.

    After feeding on a mortal you have dreams of their lost future and you see all you have taken from them. What joys have you stolen? What do you learn? Gain a Skill.

    Your vampire foresees their own end, though you the player do not know what it is. Create a Mark about knowing your own destruction. When your vampire is finally destroyed reflect on the fact that they knew exactly what was going to happen, even if you didn't.

36. Your marks are discovered and you are heralded as a saint. Check a Skill. Gain a Skill and a Resource gifted by or taken from religious practitioners who believe in you.

37. You have a brief reprieve from the forces which harass you—a year of quiet. Work on a project you've long set aside. Lose one Resource by improving it into two separate Resources. Create a mortal Character who is divisive.

Rest, recover, make peace with yourself. Take one Mark and lose it, change it, or otherwise come to terms with it. Create an older mortal who is a leader of the community you prey upon. Speak with them.

A Character holds you in contempt for doing something selfish or foolish or dangerous. What did you do and why? Gain a Resource.

38. A supernatural enemy moves against you. One close mortal Character is converted into an immortal, quasi-sentient hunting thing set to tracking you. Strike out any other living mortals on your list.

39. What's this? A head in a box? And it...it can talk? Create an immortal Character that is also a Resource. This head must be used to fill your next three needs for a Character. Where did you get this thing?

The head wants a body and you must give it one. Check a Skill.

It's time to put *your* head in the box. Go quietly or check three Skills. What's it like being a head in a box?

Ha ha, what's this new delight? Why, I could dedicate all my hours to this marvelous activity! I think I will! Gain a Skill about a foolish pastime.

Why, other people share this interest! Remarkable! Create a mortal Character who also does this thing. Lose a Resource. Change your name to something related to this fad.

You've lost focus and everything burns. Flee for a new land. Lose all stationary Resources.

Additional Prompts
by
Jessie Rainbow

41. A beloved mortal Character confesses their romantic interest in you. How do you react? How do you hide your monstrous side from them? Create a mortal Character if necessary.

> The infatuated mortal follows you into a dangerous situation and is injured. You boil with anger and punish the one responsible for their injury while the mortal watches. What changes in how the mortal sees you? Take the Skill *Heedless*.

>> The doting mortal confronts you about your immortal nature. They request you turn them, to allow you both to be together for eternity. If you agree change the mortal Character into an immortal Character, check a Skill and take the Skill *Obligated Sire*. If you refuse gain a Mark and take the Skill *Scorned*.

42. You discover an immortal and are immediately smitten. Create an immortal Character.

> You become obsessed with the immortal, following them, longing to be with them. You abandon habits and recklessly move into dangerous territories, create a Skill that reflects this.

>> Your yearning for the immortal grows, they're all you can think about. Whether you realize it or not, you begin to mimic them. Your body begins to change from your unquenching desire, take a Mark. Check a Skill.

43. A mortal Character sends you a precious gift. How is it ill-suited for your immortal lifestyle? How do you react? Gain a Resource.

> Courting rituals have changed since you first learned them. As the mortal continues to attempt to catch your eye, how do you mistake their machinations? Check a Skill.

44. You cross paths with a mortal Character from long ago. Old feelings of romantic love stir within you. Take the Skill *Hopeless Romantic*.

> The aging mortal returns your affections. Your May to December romance sweeps you off your feet. You're so caught up in it you abandon your usual feeding routines. How does your beloved react when they see your resolve weaken with hunger? Check a Skill.

>> Years slip past without you realizing. The mortal grows older, frailer, and soon becomes ill. You realize their death will be prolonged and you consider ending their misery now while they're still lucid. If you slay your beloved to keep them from suffering gain a mark and take the Skill *Heartbroken*. If you watch their illness progress and eventually consume them check a Skill and take the Skill *Haunted*.

45. Your diary is stolen. Months later you discover your most intimate passages published under a pseudonym, the story greatly aggrandized and romanticized. Lose your Diary.

> You receive pages from your diary along with a note asking you to meet with the mysterious author. What surprises you about them at the rendezvous? Do they fully understand your immortal nature? Regain two Memories from the lost diary, add them to your current Diary. If necessary the current diary can expand to hold up to six entries.

>> Through trickery you are revealed publicly as the author of the popular work. People see you as a romantic guru and they clamor for advice; some seek your guidance in a more intimate setting. How does this change your feeding patterns? Gain the Resource *Devotees*. Add a Skill you learn while entertaining these people.

Additional Prompts
by
Elizabeth Bellisario
and
Amber Autumn Faebrooke

ALTERNATE STARTING PROMPT

You are wounded and discover yourself susceptible to a classic vampire weakness. Create a Mark that embodies this weakness.

You accidentally kill someone you love using heretofore undiscovered powers. Strike out a Character. Create a Mark that embodies a classic vampire power.

You find yourself gravely wounded by something you once loved. Create a Mark that embodies a heretofore-undocumented vampire weakness.

Your body flies out of your control by a power you did not understand and you are forced away from your home for a lifetime. Create a Mark that embodies a heretofore-undocumented vampire power and cross off all mortal Characters.

You spend years training and experimenting with your body to gain as much control over it as possible. Gain a weakness (as a Mark), a Skill, a Resource, and a helpful Mark, all related to maximizing the potential of your vampiric form.

46. A Character from your past spreads rumors about you, which become half-true legends. Who does this? How do you find out? Create a Resource *Reputation*. Next to it, write 2 memories, current or forgotten, in as much detail as you, the player, can remember without looking. Your vampire is considered to "know" these things about themself through this secondhand account. Like the Diary, if this Resource is lost, so are those memories.

> You begin to lose track of what is reality and what is fiction. Do not write down an Experience for this entry; instead, if you have the Resource *Reputation,* swap one Memory your vampire has with one Memory from the *Reputation*, and if you do not have that Resource, forget one Memory.

>> The legends of you grow so outrageous that a professional vampire hunter comes for you. Create a mortal Character. How do you get away? If you have the Resource *Reputation*, move whichever Memory you place this Experience in into that *Reputation* as a third slot.

47. Your hiding place is plundered and your things are scattered through the world. Lose one Resource. Turn to any three Prompts in this book and write down a treasure or magical Resource in each Prompt. If you reach that Prompt at any point, you have found your lost treasure; gain that Resource.

> A mortal in your life finds out about you and begs you to make them like you. How do they get you to say yes? It seems, as far as you can tell, that your feeding doesn't work. Strike out one mortal Character (create a Character if necessary). Turn to any two Prompts in this book and write that Character's name there. If you reach that Prompt at any point, you discover that the process did work; unstrike that Character and make them immortal.

48. While reading, you find records of a person you're sure is you from ages past, conducting your affairs with people you can't remember. Create two mortal Characters from your past. Strike them both out immediately.

> People grow suspicious and you are forced to return to a place you used to call home. Do you know you used to live here? How is it different? Before recording this Experience, create a new Memory of two Experiences related to this place, and then immediately forget them.

49. You become ashamed of the past you no longer connect with, and go to great lengths to destroy any histories which contain you. How do you do this? Do you succeed? If you physically tear a page out of a book (an actual, physical real world book, not an in-game book), gain one Skill. If not, check a Skill.

> You become obsessed with your quest to be forgotten, actively throwing away pieces of your current life to crush your past. Lose two Resources. From now on, whenever you finish the last Prompt on a page, including this one, you may tear it out of the book and gain one Resource. If you do this, you may no longer complete any Prompts on the removed fragments, front or back.

50. You encounter an immortal Character from your past, but they no longer remember you. If there are no immortal Characters, create one. Check one Skill to gain their trust; otherwise, they regard you with suspicion.

> You and that Character spend a lifetime together. If you are feuding, check a Skill; if you are companions, lose a resource. How does this relationship end?

>> Generations pass; you and that Character encounter one another again, and again they have forgotten you. How do you treat them now? Strike out all mortal Characters. If you and the immortal Character had feuded before, gain the Skill *Ancient Grudge* and one other Skill. If you had been companions, gain the Resource *Binding Heirloom* and one other Resource.

51. You do battle, and some great injury addles your brain. Who did you fight? Mark one Memory slot "hazy"—from now on, the only words you may write in that Memory slot are verbs and adjectives.

> Your wounds make you weak, and a perfectly ordinary illness arrives to ravish your body for years. Lose one Resource. You emerge from your delirium having mixed events up in your brain. You may combine two memories into one Memory slot, even if it exceeds three Experiences in that Memory slot, but you must rewrite the first and last Experiences so that they seem to connect, though they didn't at the time.

>> You find that your body and mind recover from the sickness more monstrous and powerful than before. Gain a Mark. Mark your "hazy" Memory slot as "vast"—you may now fit two additional Experiences in that Memory slot.

52. You begin to feel that your body no longer matches the person you are, and you go to great lengths to permanently change your body to match. What do you do? Gain a Mark.

53. You find yourself in an impossibly dark place and a stranger sacrifices everything they have to do you an incredible kindness. Create a new mortal Character. What do they do for you? You swear to them that you will never forget this.

> You and that mortal Character (or their descendant, create one if necessary) have remained close confidantes. One day, they find themselves in great danger and you save their life. What do you do? Check a Skill. They swear to you they will never forget this.

>> You spend decades apart, but again encounter that mortal (or their descendant). They still remember you. Do you still remember what they, or their ancestor, did for you? If yes, give away a Resource. If not, gain the Skill *Let Everyone Down*.

54. A group of mortals discover you and treats you like a god. How do you fail them?

55. You and another immortal Character attempt to use one another as a food source. Create a new Character if necessary. How does this affect your relationship? How does it make your body both better and worse? Gain a Skill related to these bodily changes. On your next roll, reverse the dice, subtracting the d10 from the d6.

> It becomes clear that the more you feed this way, the more powerful and monstrous you become, while they become weaker and more wretched. One day they leave you forever. If they were a friendly Character, they become an enemy. Gain a Mark. On your next roll, do not roll the D10, simply move back d6 Prompts.

>> You are overcome with an insatiable need for your former food. You hunt down your prey. Check three Skills to avoid killing them. Otherwise, strike out that Character as you feed too deeply on their magical blood—on your next roll, add the D6 instead of subtracting it.

56. Disaster befalls a city you are in—disaster you have seen before. For one day you are a great hero. How do you help? Check a Skill and gain a Skill.

> You feel compelled to Experience that taste of glory again, so you strike out to find more disasters to avert and cities to save. How do you find these places? Check a Skill and gain a Skill.

>> Eventually, the easiest thing becomes causing disasters which you can be lauded for saving some people from. What carnage do you create? Check a Skill and gain a Skill.

57. Personal and cultural events collide and compel you to travel elsewhere. Where do you go? As you travel, you reinvent yourself again, and forget yourself in the process. Delete the first clause of every sentence in one Memory.

> You spend a lifetime traveling and gain a new sense of perspective. It's peaceful, and even fulfilling. You learn to center yourself. Replace all the proper nouns in one Memory with your name.

>> You spend another lifetime living in the most secluded place you can find. The rest of the world falls away from you. You are happy. Lose either your earliest Memory or three other Memories.

58. You enter into a demonic pact with a powerful immortal being; choose an existing Character or create a new one. Tribute a Resource of great personal significance. Gain the Resource *Accursed Strings*. For as long as you have this Resource, whenever you land on a Prompt, you may strike out X checked Skills, where X = the number of times you have previously landed on this page +1, to instead land on the Prompt on the previous page.

> The being you made the deal with comes to collect. If you don't still have the Resource *Accursed Strings* they kill a friendly immortal Character (or all mortal Characters, if unable). If you do still have the *Accursed Strings* they take your soul for their own. What use is your soul to them? The game is over.

59. You lose your Diary in the midst of a long journey. Desperate to find it, you tear through the distance you covered. Either lose your Diary or lose a Memory.

> Your Diary is stolen. You get it back but find that it has been vandalized, and you no longer recognize what handwriting belongs to your past self. Change all the proper nouns in 2 Diary entries to new, made-up names; change all non-proper nouns in the other entires to new, unrelated nouns.

>> You lose your Diary to global turmoil beyond your control. Either lose your Diary or lose all your other Resources to get it back.

60. You partake in communal mortal activities, such as feasts or dances, and your enjoyment is genuine. Create a mortal Character who trusts you.

> The pleasures of mortal delights consume you for some time, but eventually your body rejects them. Who is witness to this? Create an enemy mortal Character, or change an existing mortal Character to an enemy.

>> Your final encounter with one of these delights ruins it for you forever. Create a Mark that reflects your unwillingness or inability to engage with it again.

61. The first still-living Character you've met comes to fulfill a promise they made to you long ago. Do you remember them? What was the promise? Create a Skill derived from your relationship.

   The second still-living Character you've met comes to demand you fulfill a promise you made to them long ago. What was the promise? If you remember this person, check a Skill to fulfill the promise and gain a Resource they give you in reward. If you do not remember them, gain the Skill *Oathbreaker* and they take a Resource from you.

   The most recent still-living Character you've met comes to you with unconditional acceptance. How do you drive them away with your suspicion? They become an enemy Character, if they weren't already.

62. Mortals create a modernized revival of a practice you used to partake in. Create a new Skill similar to one you checked long ago, whether or not you remember it.

   The Skill is modernized beyond your recognition or current abilities, and you grow frustrated. Do you withdraw from it or attempt to guide it back to familiar territory? Check a Skill or create an enemy Character.

   You stumble upon an artifact from your past that relates to this revival. How does it shake the world? Lose a Resource and gain a Resource.

63. You are involuntarily sealed off from civilization for a lifetime. How did this happen? Strike out all mortal Characters.

   Your confinement ends due to the intervention of a mortal you do not know. How do they know of you? What do they want from you? Create a new mortal Character.

   Your rescuer threatens to expose your existence, knowingly or unknowingly. How do you deal with this threat? Lose a Resource or check a Skill.

64. You find a substitute for your current food source. How is a change in sustenance expressed in your physical appearance?
Gain a Mark and a Resource.

> Your previous food source becomes unavailable, though the substitute wasn't meant to be permanent. What do you lose from this besides food? Check a Skill or lose a Resource.

>> The substitute food source becomes problematic. Check two Skills to retain it, or lose a Resource as you struggle to find another replacement.

65. You intentionally produce a child. With whom? Create a mortal Character. Record an additional Experience about the best day you ever have with them.

> Your child grows old and dies, leaving you with a healthy lineage. Strike off your child; gain the Resource *Profane Lineage.* For as long as you have this Resource, every time you create a mortal Character, roll your d10; if it is a 0, that Character is your descendant, whether you remember that or not.

>> You are sheltered from danger by a family of your descendants for a time. Create two new Characters, one of whom is descended from you and one of whom is not. They look older than you are. In what ways do you feel they are wiser than you are?

66. You accidentally produce a child. With whom? Create a mortal Character. Record an additional Experience about the best day you ever have with them.

> Your child grows old and dies, leaving you with a healthy lineage. Strike off your child; gain the Resource *Arcane Lineage.* For as long as you have this Resource, every time you create an immortal Character, roll your d10; if it is a 1, that Character is your descendant, whether you remember that or not.

>> You strike a powerful magical being and they place a curse on you and your descendants. Create an immortal Character or use an existing one. Lose any Resources which refer to your lineage and immediately strike out any Characters who are descended from you.

67. You try to build something that will outlast you. What is it? What do you sacrifice for it? Lose a Resource.

> You live to see that thing crumble. What causes this? Gain a Skill related to this event.

>> Imitators and echoes of the original thing begin to appear around the world, with no clear way of tracing their origin to you. How do you realize this is happening?

68. Across languages and aliases, your name shifts. Where do you go that prompts the most recent change? Pick a new name that feels appropriate for who you are now and write it at the top of your Character sheet, crossing out your previous name. Include in this Experience what your previous name was.

> You meet someone who shares your former name and grow to hate them. Create a new mortal Character with that name. If you still remember this name, replace that name in your Memory with a proper noun from elsewhere in your memories. If not, replace all proper nouns in another Memory with that name.

>> That mortal uncovers the connection between the two of you and you disavow names altogether. Strike the name off of your sheet; either write in a formal title instead or leave it blank.

69. You discover that you can transform into an animal. What kind of animal? How do you use this power? Gain the Skill *Feral Transformation*.

> You spend some years living among the animals instead of among the humans. How is this easier? How is it harder? Gain a Skill related to your animal.

>> You awaken one day and realize you can't tell how long you've been living among the animals. You return, but you are different. Mark whichever Memory slot you place this Experience in "primal." From now on, Experiences you place in that slot do not contain the "what happened" sentence clause, only the "how I felt about it" clause.

70. You enslave a mortal to be your thrall as a food source, but soon you and the mortal become involved. Create a mortal Character.

> The mortal begins to take advantage of the relationship, and you find yourself under their thumb, but still caring for them deeply. What do they have you doing for them? Check a Skill.
>
> > You leave that relationship behind, and it tears you apart. Check a Skill to walk away. Otherwise, you intentionally feed too deeply; strike that Character out.

71. You return to an old home to find that any reminder of your previous residence has been thoroughly removed, either through the passage of time or through deliberate erasure. What do you do to reclaim it?

> Upon closer inspection, it seems that the mortals in this place have learned from your last stay here, although they may not realize that the traditions their ancestors have passed down were, at one time, key to survival. How do the anti-vampire structures and traditions within their society inconvenience or harm you? Lose a Resource.
>
> > Not all have forgotten the meanings behind their age-old traditions. You are careless in your reclaimed home, and its other residents attempt to claim you as well. Check three Skills to escape, or check 1 and create an enemy mortal. Write their name on three pages of this book; if you encounter Prompts on that page, assume that their pursuit of you complicates that Prompt.

72. You befriend a mortal of high status in their society. How does this benefit you? How does it complicate your ability to blend into society? Gain a Resource; check a Skill.

> You, too, become ensconced in the goings-on of the powerful. Your name and face are known across the land. Gain the Skill *Celebrity*.
>
> > Someone of power equal to yours recognizes your eccentric behavior for what it really is, and threatens to expose you. How do you escape when nations know your name and face? Gain a Mark in your attempts to withdraw incognito.

73. The next fresh blood you drink makes you horribly ill without a cause that you can find. Check a Skill to avoid being caught off guard.

The next few feedings make you ill as well, and you make plans to leave the area. Check a Skill to avoid being ill enough to botch one of the feedings; otherwise, create an enemy immortal Character.

Even far away from this area, you continue to be unable to retain blood. Lose two Resources to find a suitable method of recovery; otherwise, find a place to sleep it off, and roll a d10. On a 1 or 2, the game is over; else, you rest for a generation and awaken in better condition.

74. In your dreams, you see visions about a tumultuous event in the future of the world; a war, or a revolution, or similar moment. Gain a Skill related to that time; when your narrative reaches that point in history, if this Skill is not yet checked, record an additional Experience about using it to your advantage and gain a Resource.

You go to great lengths to prepare yourself for this future event. Gain a Skill related to these preparations. When your narrative reaches that point in history, check either this Skill or two other Skills to be unscathed.

You find yourself caught up in parallel events in the real world, and these wrack your nightmares now. Either remove an unchecked Skill from this page or forget any memories with Experiences taken from this page.

Every pictorial or plastic work
unnecessary, even if it is a monster which terrifies servi
minds, and not a sickly-sweet object to adorn the
tories of animals in human ga
sad fable of humanity.

ALTERNATE ENDING PROMPT

You intentionally withdraw to a place so secluded no one will ever find you. You stay there so long, you forget that humanity exists. What occupies your time? The game is over.

Though your body continues, a perfect machine, your mind takes in all it can and slowly crumbles to dust. What do you leave behind? The game is over.

The mortal world thoroughly destroys itself and you remain, a powerful figure standing over the wreckage. What happened? What do you do now with your time? The game is over.

You forget so much that you even forget why you never go into the sunlight. What causes you to try? How do you feel as you realize what's happening? The game is over.

You live for another 1,000 years. For now, though, you find, for a time, true peace and stability. Gain three additional permanent Memory slots, two mortal Characters, two Resources, and two Skills. Whenever you feel excited to return to the game, play with the same Character starting at Prompt 0. Any Prompts which are filled in now stay filled in for this second "season." As you enter the future, try not to worry too much about science fiction or worldbuilding - invent as it comes up and assume people remain fundamentally the same throughout.

Additional Prompts
by
Jackson Tegu

MEMORIES

74 Some traditional music artfully played by musicians flashes you back a
couple of hundred years, and things once forgotten return to you. Leave
your bookmark at your "present day" and flip back 12 pages. Play from
there, ignoring any creation or expenditure of Resources or killing of
Characters. When you cross your bookmark again, snap out of it and
return from that moment of reverie in your present day.

75. You read a historical account of something you experienced. You aren't
mentioned, but something secret and terrible done by you together with
three others is described in detail. What was done? Who do you think
broke the pact of silence? If you're without a fitting deceased mortal
Character, make up a name for the one you suspect of having revealed it.
Create a Skill based on what you did long ago.

> Trying to sniff out the long-dead traitor, your research leads you to
> a library far away. Where? You begin to research other parts of your
> life in this library, spend a dozen years reliving the past & reading
> about people living lives adjacent to your undead existence. Record this
> library as a stationary Resource.
>
> > You find a book written by someone who knew you, detailing a
> > part of your existence you may have largely forgotten, but regardless
> > feel connection to. This book counts as an extra Diary which holds
> > only that Memory. Write a new Memory which bears strong
> > resemblance to a previous memory of yours, whether forgotten or yet
> > remembered, to reflect the contents of the new volume. (This is in
> > addition to the Experience from this Prompt).

76. You overhear some mortals theorizing about human origins, about where they all come from. Given the information you can glean from your body, Skills, Memories, and Resources, where do you think you come from, since you may have forgotten your actual origins? Create a Skill about self-reflection or self-definition.

    As you continue to think about your origins, you develop a theory. How does your clarified outlook on who or what you are change how you behave night to night? Create a Skill about a code of conduct befitting your new understanding of yourself.

77. For reasons opaque to you, you wake up yesterday, and then the day before. You are going backwards in time. Why do you suspect this is so? Create a Mark to reflect this condition. Until you are somehow able to remove this Mark, instead subtract the result of the d10 from the d6, often resulting in a negative number when you move between Prompts. You retain memories of the future. Create a Skill about prescience. If you encounter events you've previously encountered, live them again exactly as they occurred before, except that when you're instructed to lose a Resource instead create one and visa versa.

78. A rare opportunity presents itself and you take it, catching an immortal unawares and dining upon them. What do they scream as you destroy and make a meal of them? Strike out an immortal Character if one is available, or give a name to the being you've now devoured. Create a Mark which makes you more alike to them, create a Skill foreign to anything you've ever encountered, and create as a Resource a potent, beautiful, frightening object they carried.

79. Disguised within a crowd, you hear a beautiful song from a tuneful mortal, telling the tale of something you did long ago. Something you still remember. Choose a Memory and create a Skill about finding peace or purpose with it.

80. An object you thought lost forever reappears in the hand of a rival or someone ill-disposed to you. Choose a Character or create one. Unstrike or create a Resource. What are they threatening to do with or to it? How do they reveal this to you?

81. You encounter someone who resembles a lover you had long ago. They're on the arm of someone who looks much like you did. Create two Characters. What do you do to or for them?

82. An instrument or tool that you recognize from years before resurfaces. Unstrike or create a Resource. Create a Character. Does the person who has it know what they have? What should it be used for? What are they doing with it?

83. While taking refuge in a modest study you encounter a book which feels familiar to you. Unstrike or create a Resource which is a book. What is the ornamentation on its cover? When you flip to a random page, what do you find?

84. You find a marvelous sword. Where do you find it? What does it look like? Create a Resource which is a sword.

85. You lose a sword. If you have an appropriate Resource, strike it out. Otherwise simply lose a sword of no import. How do you lose it?

86. You donate one of your objects to a museum. Which do you choose? Why is it of interest to them? Whom do you hope will see it? Lose a Resource which is an object. If you don't have an appropriate Resource, instead donate something you habitually wear.

87. You give one of your objects to a beggar. Create a Character. Why do they stand out to you? What do you hope they'll do with this? Lose a Resource which is an object. If you don't have an appropriate Resource, instead give the beggar something you habitually wear.

88. An artistic pursuit attracts your attention. What is it? Years pass as you casually dedicate yourself to mastering it. Strike out two or more mortal Characters who die of old age in the interim. Create a Skill about creating art.

Unable to match your output to the speed of your ideas, you start a workshop to employ others to craft partially-finished pieces in your style, under your direction, to which you then apply the finishing touches. Create this workshop as a stationary Resource. Create two Characters who work for you.

From this artistic style begins an art movement which brings you unwelcome acclaim and attention. Name the art movement. Choose or create a mortal Character to act as the public originator of this movement.

Your workshop is full of strong personalities and ambitions. Which of your students betrays you? How do they do it? Why? Choose or create a mortal Character. Check a Skill.

The artistic style is utilized by a mortal autocratic government to make their terrible messages more palatable. The workshop is seized. If you yet retain it as a Resource, strike it out now. [Cre]ate a Skill about seeing people as they are.

[Y]ou purchase at an auction one of your early works in that [o]nce-popular artistic style. Gain a Resource.

RE CASES
F INFLUENZA
ARE REPORTED

e Number of Deaths are
Reported to Health
Departments.

89. You've developed a very inconvenient allergy to something in your environment, something mortals don't tend to be allergic to. Create a Mark.

90. You discover a new part of your body. You don't know how long you've had this. What does it seem to be for? How do you think you got it? What does it look like? Create a Mark.

91. You begin shrinking. You're about a foot shorter than you were. How does this inconvenience you? Check a Skill.

    You shrink a further two feet. Create a Mark reflecting your stature. Which objects do you need to replace with smaller versions so that they remain usable by you? How do you go about replacing them? Lose a Resource, either as payment or to shoddy workmanship in the replacement.

    You're less than a foot tall. Strike the previous Mark about your stature and create a new Mark reflecting your stature. How does this change your nightly routines? Check a Skill.

92. You begin to once again resemble a human in some way. What is it? Why do you think this has occurred? If appropriate, remove a Mark.

93. One night while feasting, you suddenly realize you are wearing a mask, one which you've long mistaken for your face. You remove the mask. What do you look like underneath it? Where else have you seen the face beneath your mask? Gain the mask as a Resource. What do you do with it?

94. You've created a nest using regurgitated wood pulp and saliva. You deeply feel that it is durable and safe. Take it as a stationary Resource. What have you decorated it with?

> The time comes to lay your eggs. How do you do so? What do they look like? How large are they? How do you safeguard them? Take *Your Unhatched Eggs* as a Resource.

>> Returning to your eggs, you see that most have hatched and their inhabitants have gone. The last is having a little trouble; you help it escape the shell. What does this being look like? How does it regard you? Create an immortal Character.

95. Your body has begun to excrete some new kind of material. What is it? Where is it coming from? Create a Mark to reflect this.

96. Fanned to fear by a resurgence in the popularity of old folktales, you bloodily remove and carefully hide your heart. What container do you place it in? Where do you hide it? Take the stationary Resource *My Heart*.

97. Boredom leads you to crave novelty. You experiment with feeding on mortals in new and bizarre ways, some quite inconvenient. You find a method which vastly increases your enjoyment. Create a Skill to reflect this discovered method.

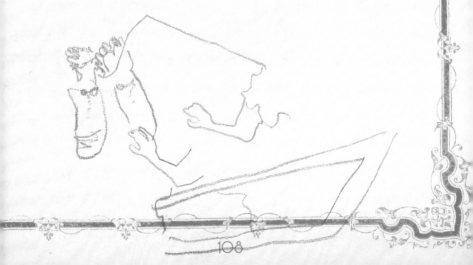

DOOM

98. After a meal which tasted strange, you discover you carry a disease which slowly kills mortals. Create a Mark to reflect this. Whenever you interact with a mortal Character, place a dot near their name. Each dot halves their remaining life expectancy.

99. The mortals here are taking some new precaution against you, something which makes their blood taste strange. Feasting upon them gives you vertigo. Some of your teeth become loose. Check a Skill and lose any stationary Resources as you escape to less proactive environs.

100. The mortals here are doing something which endangers their environment, perhaps inadvertently poisoning the water or soil. You recognize that you will suffer with them, and so undertake to stop this foolishness. Check a Skill.

101. You half-convince yourself you're no longer endangered by something which has caused you harm and vexation in times past. What causes this suspicion? You wish to experiment. Lose a Resource in the doing. Are you still endangered by that old source of harm?

102. In a mountain retreat you meet an elderly hermit and share a lengthy and enjoyable conversation. What topics are discussed? Their method for discussion and communication is clear and lovely. Create a Skill around dialogue or communication.

> You return to the elderly hermit's mountain sanctuary but they're no longer there. A different elderly hermit smiles in greeting, but the two of you don't share a language. Confused and saddened, you leave a gift. Lose a Resource.

103. Moving through woodlands, you feel drawn to a particular tree. You stay with it, get to know its rhythms and the life it supports as time spins dizzily forward. Strike out all mortal Characters.

> At some point the large, beautiful tree which you were drawn to begins to talk with you. You talk about things long gone. Create a stationary immortal Character. What else do you talk about? Check a Skill as you provide something the tree desires. What does the tree give you? Create a Resource to reflect its gift.
>
> > In your absence, some mortals have settled in the area and chopped down the tree for lumber. Of the tree they have built a large structure. What is the structure? The mortals can't hear the tree. What does the tree talk about now? Check a Skill as you influence the mortals to appropriate behavior regarding their intelligent structure.

104. Attached to a cavern or sewer system familiar to you, you find a newly made room full of mortal children with a foreign look. They are sick and fearful, most sleep. A small group approaches you. Make three mortal Characters. Check a Skill as you interact with them.

> You encounter the mortals who kept mortal children in a subterranean room. How are they familiar to you? What surprises you about them? How do you interact with them? Check a Skill.

>> Of those children once kept in a subterranean room, what have those who survived to adulthood achieved? What further hand do you have in it? Create a Skill.

105. The earth hungrily swallows you, you fall into a sinkhole. You are swept away by underground currents. Lose any Resources you weren't carrying. You spend a few years beneath the ground, trying to fit yourself through thin passages filled with rushing water. Gain a Skill. Emerge from beneath the ground years later, near a coastline.

106. You've created a nest, a collection of objects arranged in a way that brings you feelings of calm. What have you fashioned it of? What structure is it housed in? Create a stationary Resource. Give it a name. While here your loneliness and sadness can't touch you.

> You while away years in your nest. It's blissful. Create three Skills. Strike out two or more mortal Characters who die of old age.

>> You are awoken as your nest is destroyed around you. You barely escape. Lose your named nest Resource. Lose any Resources contained within it that are too large to carry. You're crushed by the loneliness and sadness rushing back in and it affects your identity. Change your Name to the name you had given your nest or a close approximation thereof.

107. On a clear, bright, night in a broad field, a small group of mortals mistake you for an otherworldly being. How do they address you? What do they ask of you? What do you do for them? Create a Skill.

> A different group of mortals, far distant, mistakes you for the same otherworldly being. How is what they ask of you different than what the previous group asked? Create a Skill. Create an immortal Character whom you've not yet met but bear some resemblance to.

108. You hear talk of some monster, folktales of another being that might be similar to you. This creature threatens to expose you by its lack of subtlety in feeding, so you shall hold it to reckoning. But first you must find it. Check a Skill. How is it similar to you? How is it different? What do they call it?

> After fruitless searching for the unsubtle beast you decide to abandon civility, take on its mindset and search deeper. Write its name next to yours and use it interchangeably with your own. How is the beast described? How does it behave? Create a Skill inspired by these things.
>
> > In a small village central to the unsubtle beast's territory, you capture a mortal who claims to have seen the beast's lair. Create a mortal Character. At your cruel insistence, the mortal takes you to the lair, a place grim and in disrepair, forgotten, abandoned these long many years since you yourself took refuge there. There is no beast. Just mortals' tales, and you. Unstrike or create a *Lair* stationary Resource.

109. Awakening one evening, you find a terrified mortal bound and left by other mortals for you to feast upon. Create a mortal Character. What kind of devil do you suppose they think you are? This behavior obviously can't be rewarded, so you unbind the mortal and ask after their captors. Check a Skill as you hunt and consume those who bound your new ward.

110. You become a butler for a family of bears who live in a cave in the woods. Create five mortal bear Characters: Brambly, Tuck, Tim, Dobkin, and Sharamaya-yasha. What do they love about you? Create a Skill about butling.

> The family of bears hosts a pie-eating competition. They ask you to be the master of ceremonies, and then at the last moment to join the competition, which you then win. What do you say to the crowd as you award yourself the blue ribbon? Create a Resource.

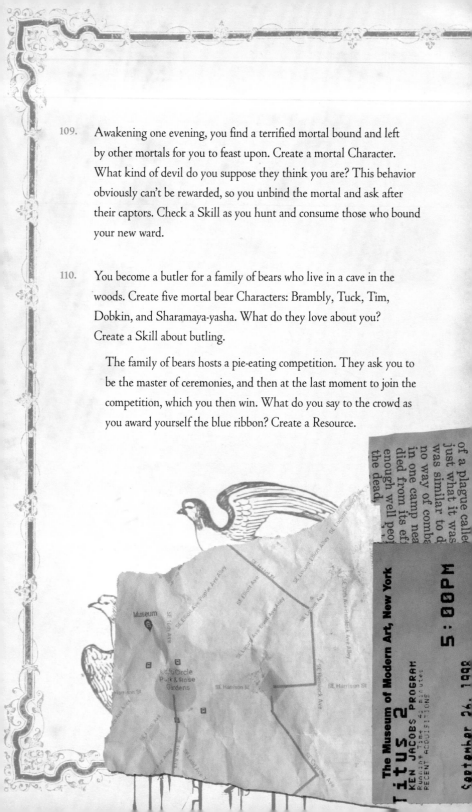

of a plague called
just what it was
was similar to d
no way of comba
in one camp nea
died from its eff
enough well peop
the dead,

111. A group of animal scavengers distantly follows you. Are they of one species, or several? How long do they wait to descend on your leavings? Create a single Character to represent this group of scavengers.

> You find the corpse of one of the animal scavengers, a few days dead. Stiffly it stands up to hop a more comfortable distance from you. This can't be left undealt with. Check a Skill.

>> You are preparing to sleep when a mortal's drunken cries reach you from somewhere outside. He is pounding at some door. There is a great scrabbling of tiny feet. You hear his screams as he is overtaken by many mouths, many beaks, many fangs. There is an epidemic of vampiric animals in this city. Check a Skill.

112. You encounter someone who follows your every verbal direction, everything you say they immediately do. They are calm while doing so, relieved, as if this is more comforting than making their own decisions. They tell you that they have no employment, no family, no hobbies or interests. Create a mortal Character. What do you bid them do?

> Your puppet reappears after a span of being uncontactable. They inform you out of nowhere that they do not wish to have children. You wonder idly if their children would carry this same agreeable trait. Create a Resource.

>> If your puppet is still alive, they are now old. They make, or you now recall them making, one request of you. What is it? Are you capable of granting it? Do you want to? Do you? Check a Skill.

113. A mortal somehow catches you unawares and, brandishing a knife, asks "what's life worth to you?" How do you confront this philosophical question, and this fool of bad judgment? Create a Skill.

114. Of late, as you draw near, animals have begun to start with fright, pitch dramatically, or flee. Which animal's actions made this clear to you? Take the Mark *Animals Fear Me*.

115. As you begin your daily ablutions, the water in your basin grows hotter. Experimenting, you remove your hand. The water cools. You return your hand to the water and it works itself to a boil, scalding you. Why would water wish you ill? Take the Mark *Water Seeks To Burn Me*.

> Preparing to read, you take a taper to the hearth with which to light your candle, but the taper refuses to light. As you squat by the fire, it burns low in the hearth, eventually dropping away to ash and coals. What will you do hereafter in place of reading? Take the Mark *Fires Extinguish Near Me*.

116. You encounter a man sewn of several corpses, but now quite capable of motion and conversation. Create an immortal Character. What do the two of you discuss? What does this being ask of you?

117. A natural spring, rumored to have curative qualities, removes some of your monstrousness. A miracle. Strike out a Mark. How does your body change? Why do you feel empty?

118. A colleague or acquaintance thinks you are an impostor without the Mark cured by the natural spring. If you don't have an appropriate acquaintance, create a mortal Character whom you've known for half a decade and momentarily forgot. How do you demonstrate you are yourself? Create a Skill.

119. A group of self-described "vampire hunters" invade your home while they presume you asleep. Make two mortal Characters and note that they are members of this group. Choose a Character whom you already knew and note that they too are a member of this group. What other trick is up their sleeve? How do you escape? Check a Skill. Lose a Resource.

> One of the so-called "vampire hunters" underestimates you, and you catch them unawares in the night. Kill a mortal vampire hunter Character. They have with them a small kit containing a variety of things which may or may not prove dangerous to you. It's so novel you find yourself unwilling to destroy it. Take the Resource *Vampire Hunter's Kit*, and note that if you ever lose track of this, you must at that time choose or create a mortal Character and note them as a vampire hunter, someone who picked up the proverbial and literal torch.

120. Someone has taken out advertisements that they want to live forever. Due to boredom, pity, or cruelty, you seek them out. Who do they tell you they are? Why do they wish to live forever? Create a mortal Character. Explain to them what your constant proximity to death feels like. Kill a mortal Character, doesn't have to be them.

121. You've seen enough ages of humankind coming and going that you can feel them like changes in the weather. How would you describe the age that is now ending? How about the next one beginning? Create a Skill.

122. You notice gradually repeating patterns in how fire burns wood, how snow falls. The world is only so complicated, only so random. Create a Skill.

123. A harsh storm season changes the shape of the human settlement you reside in. How does it change? How does the change impact your habits? Create a Skill.

> The chaos brought by the storm means that feeding becomes very easy for a while. People are lost, confused, resourceless, and easy prey. Create a Resource.
>
>> Some humans, now shelterless, take up residence in your dwelling. Do you flee or cohabitate? Check a Skill.

124. You hide for a time in a temple, church, or other holy place. Create a Skill based on stealth. Unseen, what do you witness?

> While in the temple, church, or holy place, you are somehow mistaken for a holy person. Someone confides in or confesses to you. Create a mortal Character. What secret yearnings do they reveal to you? Who have they wronged?

125. You attend a funeral for someone you've not met in person. Why are you here? Who were they? An inconsolable someone asks you to speak before those gathered. What do you say?

> Some time later, you see the deceased person whose funeral you attended. They're ambulatory, dressed well, holding a piece of fruit and staring at it thoughtfully. How have they changed? What topics do you speak on together? Create an immortal Character.
>
>> You and the immortal Character whose funeral you attended together attend another funeral. Strike out a mortal Character, or if you haven't one, make up a name for the deceased. Someone asks you to speak. What do you say?

126. You find yourself attending a very fancy ball, masked. There are people and things on display there too beautiful not to claim as your own. Create a Character. Create a Resource. Who was this person up until tonight? How do they become yours? And what does the object you take mean to its previous owners?

127. You have grown despondent in your workings. Lose a Skill. Though you are sloppy and careless, fate conspires to keep you alive. How does your unlife nearly end, and how are you saved? If you're feeling spiritual, create a voiceless, formless, imperceptible immortal Character. If you're not feeling spiritual, chock it up to luck.

128. Something that used to be difficult is extremely easy for you now. You do it without thinking at all. What is it? Create a Skill for this incredible unthinking proficiency.

129. You see a wretch, cast off from society. What do they look like? You decide to improve their lot in life. How do you go about it? Check a Skill.

130. Pursued by someone, you lose them and hide in the mud at the bottom of a river. Some hours later, young lovers arrive to romance one another and swim. Their feet brush you. How do you respond? Check a skill.

    If one or both die, you quietly attend the funeral. If they lived, you quietly attend their wedding. In either case among those gathered you recognize something about human group relationships which you'd never noticed before. What is it? Create a Skill about social perception.

131. You are unknowingly transported like cargo as you slumber. Who might have moved you? You awaken an uncertain amount of time later, somewhere entirely foreign. Lose all Resources you didn't keep on your person. What can you see around you? Trees, perhaps?

132. You gradually realize that someone who has long been part of your existence is a figment of your imagination. Perhaps they died long ago, or perhaps they never existed. You'll never know for sure. Choose a Character or make one. Even though you realize this, they still show up where you usually see them & talk with you. How do you take this realization? What do you say to them?

133. A solitary vermin starts living in your body. You feel glad for its presence, its tiny sounds. It cuts through the loneliness. What is it? Where does it live in you? Make a mortal Character.

> You can feel yourself making choices to make the vermin's life easier, even when those choices make your own life more difficult. Check a Skill. What choices do you make?

> > One day while you're walking across a room the vermin takes control of your body and never gives it back. Lose all Skills with a mental or social focus. From now on, only gain physical Skills. Lose any Resources far distant or whose purpose is unclear to someone besides yourself, including your Diary. The mortal vermin has become immortal. From now on, play as two characters: the prisoner, who has long acted but now only witnesses and remembers, and the vermin, of alien mind, who controls the body's movements for its own opaque but slowly revealed goals.

134. You see something incredibly beautiful, some moment of serendipity. Perhaps between two mortals, perhaps one mortal encountering something, perhaps just something in the world. What do you see? You feel something when you see it. What do you feel? After you decide, know that you'll remember this forever: as you write an experience of this time, put a box around it. Even if the Memory containing this Experience fades, you'll never lose this Experience—keep it forever and do not count it toward your Memory limits.

135. One night you find yourself seized with the desire to communicate to mortals how it feels to exist like this, to be pulled helplessly through time, passions long extinguished, constantly witnessing everything wilting. Come up with a sketch for an activity or reference that might communicate to a mortal how immortality grinds one's selfhood to flour. Create a Resource. Leave the sketch incomplete.

APPENDIX

II

RANDOM NUMBERS

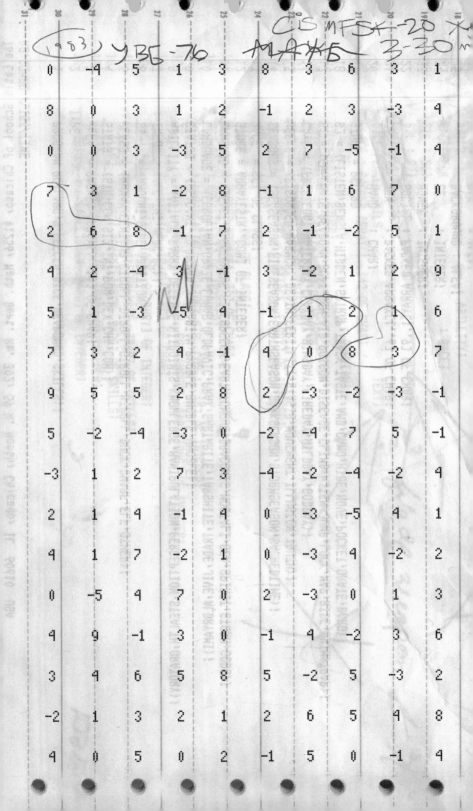

1983 УБ-76 CIS MFSK-20 X МАЯК 3-30

31	30	29	28	27	26	25	24	23	22	21	20	19	18
0	-4	5	1	3	8	3	6	3	1
8	0	3	1	2	-1	2	3	-3	4
0	0	3	-3	5	2	7	-5	-1	4
7	3	1	-2	8	-1	1	6	7	0
2	6	8	-1	7	2	-1	-2	5	1
4	2	-4	3	-1	3	-2	1	2	9
5	1	-3	-5	4	-1	1	2	1	6
7	3	2	4	-1	4	0	8	3	7
9	5	5	2	8	2	-3	-2	-3	-1
5	-2	-4	-3	0	-2	-4	7	5	-1
-3	1	2	7	3	-4	-2	-4	-2	4
2	1	4	-1	4	0	-3	-5	4	1
4	1	7	-2	1	0	-3	4	-2	2
0	-5	4	7	0	2	-3	0	1	3
4	9	-1	3	0	-1	4	-2	3	6
3	4	6	5	8	5	-2	5	-3	2
-2	1	3	2	1	2	6	5	4	8
4	0	5	0	2	-1	5	0	-1	4

4	7	0	0	1	-3	0	9	-2	2
3	1	5	-1	-4	2	2	-1	0	5
7	6	4	-4	-1	5	2	-1	2	1
4	0	6	7	2	3	1	1	5	0
5	0	2	5	6	1	1	3	-3	-1
-1	3	2	6	-4	-1	1	4	6	-5
0	6	1	3	7	0	0	1	0	6
6	-2	7	-2	3	2	4	2	8	3
2	5	2	4	1	4	1	0	0	5
6	-1	3	6	9	-2	-2	3	4	-1
-1	-1	0	-4	1	4	0	8	8	-2
4	-1	3	6	3	0	-5	5	2	0
-3	-2	-2	-2	3	1	3	3	6	-3
1	3	5	4	-2	3	7	6	3	4
-4	1	4	-4	2	8	5	-1	6	4
6	-2	5	3	-1	-3	4		-3	5
2	0	9	0	5	-1	5	6	4	7
2	2	3	0	5	1	-3		4	7

-3	9	3	6	3	9	-4	-4	-3	6
0	-2	-3	-1	1	2	-1	0	5	-3
3	9	2	1	2	2	-2	2	6	0
-4	5	-1	0	3	-1	5	3	1	5
0	3	-1	1	-2	4	2	1	3	0
-1	0	0	-1	7	8	5	-2	4	4
0	-2	1	-5	2	1	0	-2	0	1
-2	1	8	-1	4	-3	0	-1	5	8
8	1	7	2	3	-1	0	-2	8	5
4	2	3	3	7	4	7	4	1	7
2	8	2	4	8	3	-2	3	-2	2
6	-5	0	-3	6	1	4	4	4	-3
4	3	-1	1	1	-1	2	0	-1	-1
4	-3	-3	-3	-5	-1	4	0	-5	-2
0	9	-1	2	6	-3	-3	-1	5	3
4	3	2	3	4	1	3	0	0	-1
-1	-1	7	3	5	5	6	6	7	3
4	-2	2	5	5	5	4	3	5	4

Ohio - BLK 6

1	3	3	4	5	4	1	-1	7	-3
3	7	6	6	4	1	4	7	3	3
-3	3	0	0	6	5	-5	1	-4	9
3	-3	4	0	2	2	5	2	1	9
3	-2	7	5	-2	-4	2	0	1	5
1	-5	1	6	3	-1	5	-4	6	1
4	-2	-4	2	0	-2	1	-1	2	4
4	6	0	-2	6	8	6	6	3	1
4	1	8	2	1	5	-1	4	0	0
-4	1	1	-4	-2	6	4	-4	0	-2
4	5	2	4	3	1	5	7	6	1
4	2	8	0	4	1	7	0	0	-1
-2	7	-4	7	3	-1	1	2	2	0
-4	6	2	7	5	2	2	0	6	3
3	2	1	2	4	4	2	5	-1	0
3	7	-1	2	-2	5	0	8	-1	-3
6	5	8	5	2	5	3	-2	-2	0
5	6	-3	-1	-3	1	7	-2	6	2

-3	9	3	6		
0	-2	-3	-1		
3	9	2			
-4	5	2			
0	3	-1			
-1	0	0			
0	-2	1			
-2	1	8			
8	1	7			
4	2	3			
2	8	2			
6	-5	0	-3		
4	3	-1	1		
4	-3	-3	-3		
0	9	-1	2		
4	3	2	3		
-1	-1	7	3	5	6
4	-2	2	5	5	4

1. Springfield (Missouri) *News*, July 29, 1940.

Upon Christ's grave three roses bloom,
Stop, blood, stop!

Donald county, Missouri, simply neid up both hands and cried:

MYSTERIOUS FOG IN MEUSE

DISPERSED BY SUN AFTE

SCORES OF DEATHS IN

STRANGE MALADY
FOLLOWS HEAVY
MIST IN VALLE

(From Yesterday's Final Edition)

Brussels, Dec. 5.—(AP)—Fifty-eight men have died in lages scattered along the Meuse valley in Belgium from so strange malady which seems to have stricken them from out the heart of a dense fog in which the district has been shroud for the past three days.

Cattle also have been affected by this strange malady of the mist and many of them have died. Today frightened and bewildered farmers drove as many as possible of their cows and horses into warm dry kitchens to shield them from the death outside.

One theory of the mysterious malady is that it has resulted from a leak of poison gas from some unknown source which mixed with the fog in the Meuse valley and

drifted down the air currents.

Members of the public hea committee at Brussels, immediat upon hearing the report of deaths, proceeded to Engis for investigation.

Most of the deaths were at En where 14 persons succumbed. the Liege district itself eight dead at Flamalle Haute, four Flamelle Grande, five at Y Ramet, 10 at Jemeppe-Sur-Me and seven at Othee.

Late News Flashes

AND
YOU

12
new york city

Appendix Three

A Non-Verbal Affirmative Consent Tool for Narrative Play by Tayler Stokes, adapted for solo play with Tim Hutchings.

On the following page spread you will find a flower with yellow petals circling a red center surrounded by green leaves labeled with emotional and physical descriptors. Use this to track your play experience as you play by...

> *...noticing when you are experiencing something described on the flower and...*

> *...making a dot in the colored area that corresponds to your experience and...*

> *...recording the current chapter number next to the dot and...*

> *...continue working your way around clockwise adding dots and chapter numbers as you notice your responses to play and...*

> *...connect the dots with lines as you go making a chart of your play experience.*

Take a moment every couple of Prompts to gaze upon the flower and reflect on your play experience. Add dots and notes accordingly, but don't worry if you aren't finding your experience described on the flower - not everyone's will be. Try to notice some patterns as you go. Review your tale as needed. This will help you have more fulfilling play.

How often are you in the green?

What do those chapters have in common? See what you can do to steer your story toward similar moments. If you are in the green most of the time then things are going well.

How often are you in the yellow?

These moments often describe deeply engaging play experiences. For some people having a roughly equal mix of greens and yellows describes their peak play experience. Listen to your instincts for what is working best for you.

Are you dipping into the red?

Play experiences in the red indicate that you should probably be aware of and steer away from these moments. What can you learn from these experiences? If you've gone into the red more than a couple times, are you sure you're enjoying yourself? Consider taking a break.

Once you're done playing, review your play experience by tracing your path across the flower and skimming the chapters you made note of. Which moments do you remember the most clearly? Does your charted experience reveal something you didn't already know?

I feel...

Someone should make a movie out of this!

My braeathing changed

...disconnected and disengaged

...my breathing is constrained

I was absorbed by this moment

I can't write fast enough!

...fear or anxiety

...ridgety and restless

My braeathing changed

That was so

I recognise my personal experience

I'm feeling relaxed and comfortabl

...stiff and numb

distracted and and or forgetful

...distracted and and or forgetful

I'm feeling for the character right now

...my heart rate is increasing

I'm curious about what happens next

...tension in my body

I lost track of time

I'm grinning like a fool

Appendix Four

Five Or So Questions About
Thousand Year Old Vampire

an interview by Brie Sheldon for Thoughty

Tell me a little about* Thousand Year Old Vampire. *What excites you about it?

Well, first let me say that I don't often get excited about things I make. I get nervous, nauseous, pent up. I used to joke about the "sweat test"; if I wasn't sweating when I showed something to someone I wasn't sufficiently invested in the project or the showing. This came out of the time when I was showing art in galleries, and it has something to do with the way I made and thought about art at the time. It still applies to a lot of games I make, but in a different way--the games I make are personal, or visceral, or difficult in ways that my art never was. Now I sweat because I'm making a machine that people play with, and if the manual for that machine is unclear people will break it or maybe even get hurt. There's not a lot of room for excitement in any of this.

But I'm excited about *Thousand Year Old Vampire* in a way that leaves me quietly alarmed at myself. I've worked on this game differently

than other games, with the biggest difference being that a reaching back to my old studio process. When I made a thing in the studio it was a quick, fraught process during which I could ingest or enjoy or experience the thing I was making it as it was made; the actual "artwork" was a shell left behind after this work was done. Game making is different in that you need people or systems to test things; there's a space of time between the making and the experiencing of it. Because *TYOV* is a solo game it's making was a self-contained process, I wrote and played and wrote and played in a closed system. It was fast and amazing and it's how I want to be.

And it produced a game I am excited for and proud of. I've played this game so many times, and the prompts consistently produce a different experience with every go. And at least once during each game something happens that makes my innards churn, something unexpected and awful and it's like I'm not controlling a character but being betrayed by one. I'm not a "let me tell you about my character" kind of person, but *TYOV* has gotten me excited enough to write game summaries on the Facebooks.

What is the motivation for a single-player game like this? As someone who loves lonely games and making them, I must ask: why is this game good alone?

I love your phrasing of "lonely games"! It's perfect. For me, there were a couple of reasons to make a solo game. Maybe more than a couple.

Solo games are a weird design space. I have a print out of *A Real Game* by Aura Belle that I've been sitting on for a year, I'm so excited about it I can't bear to play it. Every game I make is about communication and bodies in space; a framework for people pushing at each other to find play. Other players change the game space for each other with a constant barrage of gentle tugs which keep each other engaged and off-center— this is awesome and good but what if we didn't do that?

A non-social game is tricksy and strange. How can you operate in the "story game" space and not have it be a choose your own adventure book? The game prompts in *Thousand Year Old Vampire* make you look inward for responses, you are building something between you and the machine of the game without any other conscious actors in the room. There's no "yes and" here, oh mortal. And without other people in the room watching I can do things that I might not do otherwise when I ask questions and give horrific answers.

And the solo play echoes the subject of the game itself. You play a vampire who sees everything they love turn to dust. Your character is alone, you are alone, the two states echo each other. One play option is to keep a diary as you play. Journaling is a usually a thing you do alone. One of my objectives as a designer is to have the system and the setting inextricably bound together, so solo play works.

That said, I don't see any reason that a person can't play it with others. Why not share a pool of Characters and let the prompt reactions affect the world that the players occupy? The system is simple enough that players can do this if they want, and I'm sure some will—there's been a remarkable amount of pushback over the idea of a solo game being a thing at all.

And practically speaking: I'm a lonely guy. Making a game I can play and iterate on my own is helpful. It echoes the prevalence of solo rules in wargame design—I'm the kind of person that can't get people together to play things, so I'll make the sort of things I can enjoy on my own.

Finally: I had a conversation with Jackson Tegu, who has a solo experience called *I Was Once Like You*, that helped me think about the solo play-ness of *TYOV*. In the friendly discussion-like thing we were doing I came up with "Petit Guignol" as a term that I thought fit *TYOV*. It literally means "tiny puppet" in French and has a direct connection to the "Grand Guignol" which was a style of bloody, horrifying, naturalist theater developed in the 1890s. As I play *TYOV* I sometimes play with scale in my mind, imagining the scenes happen in the space between my arms as I update the character sheet on a keyboard. It's a play space I don't think I can imagine with other people in the room, it's tiny and close and personal. Anyways, there's that.

Tell me about the design process. The way you handle moving through the prompts is simple but clever, and you have these memories and experiences that are created. How did you develop these aspects of the game?

My design process is a sham. I stare into space until my unconscious gets bored and gives me something that I can think about, and then maybe that becomes a game, or a joke, or an artwork. My games are not the product of rigorous engagement with discourse, they are random stuff that vaguely imitates a category of thing which I understand exists in the world. These are the "Sunday painter" equivalent of game design, if that Sunday painter just really liked wearing smocks and berets but never bothered to go to a museum.

I don't design these games so much as find them laying around my brain-house. I pick them up and wipe the muck off, maybe paint them a different color to assuage a conscience that demands at least a semblance of effort, then I scribble my name on them and puff up with self-satisfaction.

But a serious aside: I don't read a lot of games, and I do this on purpose. I'm more likely to solve a problem in a useful way if I'm not clouded up with other people's solutions for similar issues. This is a good methodology unless you're building bridges or stuff where people can die. This builds on my greatest strength, which is that I'm pretty dumb.

Occasionally these magical brain-gift games might need some rough corners polished up. With *TYOV* I had to figure out a way to progress through the prompt sequence so as to maximize replayability. (You, dear reader, haven't played this game, so super quick summary: You roll some dice and slowly advance along a list of prompts which you answer about how your vampire continues its existence. If you land on the same prompt number more than once, there are second and third tier prompts you encounter. The game ends when you reach the end of the list.) By using a d6 subtracted from a d10, it created the possibility of skipping entries, of going backwards, and of landing on the same entry number more than once. This meant that rare and super rare results could easily be baked into the chart structure—you have the same chance of landing on any given number as you progress through the prompts, but there are diminished chances of landing on a number twice and getting the second-tier prompt. Landing on a number a third time usually happens once per game, and those rare third-tier prompts can be world-changing.

The tiered prompt system naturally evolved into a mini-story arc system. I can make the player introduce a self-contained Character or situation with a first-tier prompt, and in the second-tier prompt them interact with what they created in a new way. It's perfectly fine if they never hit that second tier prompt, they won't for most entries, but if they do it will naturally make a little story. It's so satisfying and it's all part of the same system, no additional rules are needed to support it.

One aspect of *TYOV* I've been thinking hard about is player safety. What are appropriate safety tools for solo play? What tools allow us to think terrible, soul souring thoughts but then put them behind us? I'm a fan of X-card-like thinking, and was around Portland while Jay Sylvano and Tayler Stokes were working on their own support signals systems. Stokes later developed the affirmative consent-based support flower, and is giving me guidance on my solo safety thinking.

One of my imperatives as a designer is getting rid of non-vital things. This is practical because additional complexity usually makes a game less fluid and harder to learn. If I can get by with three rules that's great, but if I'm going to have eight then I might as well have a hundred. Not that there's much wrong with games that have a hundred rules, I like those too. I've recently been converted to *Combat Commander*, of all things.

Something I threw out of *TYOV* are rules about tracking time. At one point I had a system in place for tracking the date. I mean, if the game is called *Thousand Year Old Vampire* then you want to know when a thousand years go by, right? But there was no benefit to tracking the actual year, it was easier to allow the player to just let the passage of time be loosely tracked in their answers to the prompts. Maybe an arc of prompts happens over a year in your head, maybe a whole generation goes by—the game works regardless. The only rule about time is "every once in a while strike out mortal Characters who have probably died of old age."

Finally, I should acknowledge the importance of *Burning Wheel* and *Freemarket* to *Thousand Year Old Vampire*. Writing good Beliefs in *Burning Wheel* is a skill, and the idea of tying character goals mechanically to the game was mind-blowing. *Freemarket* has Belief-like-ish Memories, which are something that have game mechanical effects AND can be manipulated as part of play. Both of these mechanics had outsized influence on the way I thought about Memories in *TYOV*.

Memories in *TYOV* are everything that your vampire is. You have a limited number of Memories, and every Memory is made up of a limited number of Experiences. Every Prompt you encounter generates a new Experience which is tagged onto the end of a new Memory. Eventually you run out of space for Memories, so you older Memories to a Diary. You can and will lose our Diary, along with all the Memories in it, and it's awful. But the Diary is just a stopgap anyways, as you are forced to forget things to make room for new Experiences.

Eventually you have an ancient, creaky vampire who doesn't remember that he was once a Roman emperor, or that they used to live on a glacier, or that he fell in love two hundred years ago. But they at least know how to use a computer and are wrestling with the fact that the hook-up site they used to find victims was just shut down and how will they eat now? This design goal was crystallized when I read "The Vampire" by Ben Passmore in *Now 3* put out by Fantagraphic Books. It's a heartbreaking, sad story in which you see the vampire as a deprotagonized system of habits. It's great.

What has the development of this game been like, from original inspiration to the speed of production?

This game flowed out quickly and mostly easily. My pal Jessie Rainbow I were playtesting and iterating the game over weeks instead of months. The game is built from a story games mindset and there aren't any ridiculously novel mechanics that need to be explained; I hand the rules over to a playtester and they understand them immediately and the game works.

The game works and a year of refinement to get it five percent better isn't worth it. It's done, and like an artwork it might be slightly flawed but that's part of the thing itself. I don't necessarily want an extruded, sanitized perfect thing; instead I have, like an artwork, a piece that becomes a record of it's own making. If I work on this game another year it won't get better, it'll just get different—2019 Tim will have different priorities than I do right now and all that's going to happen is that *TYOV* will torque around to reflect that. I might as well let 2018 Tim have his moment and give 2019 Tim new things to worry over.

In regards to the themes of mortality and memory, as well as with aspects of queerness in some of the prompts, how do you relate to TYOV? How is it meaningful to you?

This is hard to talk about. I think I need to break this question down into three very separate categories: My understanding of evil, personas shifting over time, and a vampire-shaped *momento mori*.

The game is twined up in my own ideas of person-scaled evil which is based on my experience of social predators, thoughtlessly selfish idiots, and rich people exerting power over others. This evil is written into the "Why did you do that awful thing you did?" type prompts, which assign an evil deed which must be justified. There's an important subtext in the game which I never say out loud: As the vampire is writing in their diary are they telling the truth? But the evil is about the wickedness that people do to each other, and this is my chance to pick out a version of it that I seldom see represented.

Completely unrelated to the themes around evil are the ideas of shifting identities. Over the centuries the vampire will be reinventing themselves so they can fit in with the societies shifting around them. As a cishet white guy I'm outside of the dialogues that happen around LGBTQA+ folks, but I see folks change over time and it's exciting. A related prompt might draw attention to ingrained societal mores that can now be abandoned because the culture of your mortal years is centuries dead. I can gently make a space for this even if I don't have that experience, with the understanding that my understanding isn't necessarily another's understanding of the space that needs to be made. Like I said before, this becomes a portrait of 2018 Tim thinking through difficult issues using creative work—this isn't Truth with a capital T.

The shifting personas of the vampire are probably the most personally resonant aspect of the game for me. I have some pretty distinct phases in my life where I was having to be markedly different people. In NYC I used to exhibit art with a gallery owned by the son of billionaires. I'd get taken to a dinner that might cost more than I made in a week then go back to my home which had holes in the floor which I could see my neighbors through. I remember hanging drywall in the morning and meeting a Rockefeller descendant later that night; he got noticeably upset that I had a scratch on the back of my hand then shut me out when I said it happened "at work." I learned that I had to keep these worlds very, very separate. And it went both ways, I found myself being reminded of the experimental filmmaker Jonas Mekas telling a story about how no one in his Brooklyn neighborhood believed him when he told them he was teaching at NYU.

Now I'm a guy with a kid living in a suburban neighborhood in Portland, Oregon. I'm not the same person that I was five years ago in New York. I can't be the same person, that guy couldn't live this life.

Which leads me to my final bit: I did things that sound wonderful and which I can't remember, I apparently did things that are terrible which I am glad I forgot. These moments are lost until someone else remembers them for me or I happen upon some chance evidence. My memory is going, and it's awful—there's a much more exciting version of me which is being forgotten. I can see my brain failing in other ways; sometimes I leave out a word when I'm writing now. I bet I did it within the text of this interview.

This loss of skill, of memory, of personality are reflected in the way the game has you lose or edit memories. Eventually I'll die and be forgotten in turn, but at least I'll have this self-reflection on mortality outlive me for a bit.

©T 22-2018

Thousand Year Old Vampire *Arises*

an interview by Sean Hillman for EN World

Tim Hutchings is putting out a game about playing a Thousand Year Old Vampire called, ironically enough, Thousand Year Old Vampire. *EN World talked to Tim about his history of game design and* Thousand Year Old Vampire *itself.*

Sean Hillman (SH): Tim, before we get into Thousand Year Old Vampire, can you tell folks about how you got into gaming and game design? What were the biggest influences?

Tim Hutching (TH): I'm one of those people who can say "I first played RPGs when I was seven or so and never stopped." Games, all sorts of games, are an important part of my life. It kills me that I don't get to play enough games, and especially that I don't get to play enough weird games.

The important shift, though, happened in my 20s in NYC. I was doing art stuff there, showing in galleries and trying to solve the world's problems by making efficacious objects. I started applying my art thinking to games, and this meshed nicely with my introduction to story gaming through NerdNYC. There I was introduced to games like the *Shab-al-Hiri-Roach* and *The Mountain Witch* and spent years playing *Burning Wheel*. These games made me want to be in the play world more than the art world. I left NYC and artmaking to come to Portland, Oregon. Here I easily slid into game making with the support of the now-defunct Game Garden design group. I'm mostly making freeform RPG/larps and simple little card games now.

SH: Talk to us about your Golden Cobra! Did winning have an affect on how you designed games moving forward?

TH: The Golden Cobra Challenge is a themed game design get-together built around freeform gaming. If it's not exactly a larp or an RPG or a board game then it's maybe a freeform. It was founded by Evan Torner and Jason Morningstar with help from Emily Care Boss, Whitney "Strix" Beltrán, Kat Jones, and Steve Segedy.

My first submission was a game about school shootings called *Active Shooter*, it was given an Honorable Mention. My second submission was a game about arguing crows called *A Crow Funeral*. That won a Best Use of Touch; players make a "handstack" in the middle of their group which controls who can talk at any given moment. I won another honorable mention for *It's All Good*, a game about the stories families tell about their ancestors. I submitted another game this year called *Egg-Eating Rabbits* which is about rabbits that eat eggs. I doubt that one will get any kind of award.

The Golden Cobras are sort of an embodiment of the awesomeness of a good vibe. The whole thing is supportive and positive and made of high fives. It's not competitive, it's a challenge, which is awesome. The awards are announced at Metatopia and then the winning games are played at the con--how cool is that? "Pretty cool" is the answer.

SH: What were the difficulties, if any, in making a game like *Dear Leader*?

TH: *Dear Leader's* big challenge was how to coat an incredibly serious subject in a fun candy shell. I wanted to make a game that would lure people in for the fun, but leave them with experiences that helped them better understand the real horrors of dictatorships. This experience can be crafted in a game like nowhere else, but it was hard to get it just right.

There was also the difficulty of being a white American commenting on the difficulties of a people far away. To help offset this I sought out folks with a direct investment in the subject matter; their insider feedback helped me ensure the game was respectful and effective. Mighty powers took an interest in my game and put it in front of North Korean refugees who gave input on it.

And then there were practical finishing issues, and those were all on me. I'd never worked on an actual boxed game before and everything took much longer than I expected. So much longer. Part of the delay came from new opportunities only made available after the Kickstarter was public, following up on these made the game better but kept pushing the schedule back. But also,

I messed up. I kept fiddling with the game and spent a year making it 5% better when I should've just delivered it. I learned a big lesson and won't do that again.

SH: What was the moment where you said "I want to make a vampire RPG"? Is this a project that has been on your mind for a while or something fairly recent?

TH: I never thought I'd make a vampire game. I'm not a vampire kind of guy. But the whole thing resolved itself in my mind so quickly that I never had a chance to say no.

Vampires are uniquely suited to the themes I wanted to deal with: Memories lost to the centuries, burying oneself beneath layers of persona, and horrible, selfish decisions being made by a character that the player doesn't quite control. I had this stuff idly spinning in my mind when I read " "The Vampire" by Ben Passmore, a comic in *Now 3* (a comic compilation). I was like, oh heck, this is exactly the feel I want; the subject is a vampire and not dreadful European iron-fearing fairies.

SH: The design cycle for *TYOV* seems pretty quick? What is the inspiration for such a quick turn around?

TH: It's way quick. So quick. Maybe too quick, but I'm cool with that.

When I was making art I did it in a way that was quick and fluid. I would work on a thing and look at it and change it and then maybe I was done. The objects I made might have flaws, but the flaws became a portrait of the making. *Thousand Year Old Vampire* recaptures that mode of artmaking: It's intuitive and dirty and incredibly personal. It might have some flaws but those aren't problems so much as thumbprints.

That, and I've learned that a year of revisions can make something 5% better, but even better than that 5% is making three totally new projects in that same amount of time.

SH: *Thousand Year Old Vampire* is a solo RPG. What about doing a solo RPG excites you? Were there specific games or influences that convinced you to choose a more asymmetrical path.

TH: Brie Sheldon used the best term "lonely games" and I think that's absolutely perfect for *Thousand Year Old Vampire*. It's a game about being an alpha predator surrounded by those you feed on. It's a game about being alone that you play alone and that's perfect.

I can point backwards at the tradition of solo wargames which fascinated me so much in the 80s and 90s. Some of the best games of that type become story generators, like Richard Berg's *Blackbeard* by Avalon Hill. Wargames needed solo rules because there weren't nearly as many gamers back then, and because so many wargames were designed as a puzzle you solve rather than a game you played.

There's a draw for me toward solo games as I'm a pretty lonely guy, I think. It's also a difficult area for me to think about as most of my games are about channels of communication

and breaking them, a lonely game is the opposite of that.

SH: The Diary and Memories play a big part in the game as do Experiences. These concepts feel like the core of the game. How do you hope the player will interact with the Diary and their memories on an emotional level, if indeed that is a goal?

TH: Memories are the core of the game. They are built around the framework of Beliefs in *Burning Wheel* and, uh, Memories in Freemarket--they are concise summaries of a moment, a single sentence that distills the importance of an event.

In *Thousand Year Old Vampire* you have five "slots" for Memories, and each Memory is made up of up to three Experiences. Every prompt you resolve generates a new Experience you have to add to one of your Memories. This forces the players to find continuity between moments in the vampire's life as they tie Experiences one to the other; it's a natural guide for story generation--"Oh, I have a prompt here about something I desire being stolen and it seems like a natural tie in with a Memory describing a mortal lover who abandoned me. Yeah, they definitely stole that symbolic key to the Vatican Archives I received when I was a Cardinal. I wonder why they'd do that?"

Over the course of the game you run out of space for Memories. New Memories force existing Memories out of your head; you can write a few down in a Diary but even that will fill up. "What will you choose to forget?" becomes a major decision in the game. You will forget your birth name, your homeland, your parents, your first love, your dog, everything...

Diaries are a mechanical way to store additional Memories, but they can be lost or stolen. As a chronic sketchbook keeper and dabbling archivist, losing a Diary is awful.

SH: Do your own experiences with memory and mortality factor into the design of *TYOV*?

TH: Yeah. I've watched people's minds sicken and die and it is heartbreaking. This game is a *momento mori*, of a sort, as I watch my own brains get soft and forgetful. I have a couple of marker experiences I can reach out and touch that remind me that this is dreadful and sad and to not forget that.

SH: Do you foresee this as something players will play by themselves and compare notes with their friends or perhaps even something a player might do with others watching? Even though it is a solo game, might there be opportunities for groups to play together as the vampire?

TH: *<Looks left, looks right, drops voice to a low whisper>* If I didn't make multiplayer rules then people would just do it on their own because that's what gamers do. The jerks.

I'm going to be at Metatopia testing multiplayer rules. The structure will be each player guiding their own vampire through the centuries.

Players can answer prompts out loud for the table or silently, to themselves. There will be a shared pool of NPCs that all the Characters interact with. Actual direct PC to PC interaction will be minimal, though, it's definitely not an "adventuring party of vampires" type thing.

My main playtester, Jessie Rainbow, and I would watch each other play the game through Google docs. We'd watch each other's character sheets change and grow and accumulate Memories then see the hard decisions get made. I never would've thought I'd get that wrought up watching a spreadsheet update.

SH: The relationships built through the game, with various characters and memories, how important will they be to the vampire's journey?

TH: The NPC Characters are very important, but the mortal Characters are also ephemeral. You might only have a mortal around for two or three prompts, certainly not more than five or six. You'll get bound up in the importance of these people and then they'll just be gone.

Immortal NPCs are almost always going to be enemies, so they are present when needed but they aren't ever going to be pleasant. It's not uncommon to have your vampire re-encounter an immortal NPC but not actually have any extant Memories of them. That's always a favorite moment of mine.

The Prompts drag these NPCs into your vampire's life in interesting ways, allowing them to boomerang in and out as needed. There the NPCs become complicated and develop personalities and relationships and then they go away, maybe forever. It's awesome and sad, and no one is acting out this NPC for you but you are just figuring out what they did and how it affected your vampire. For me it has been making a more intense interest in these NPCs because they float in an undefined abstraction.

SH: Where did the Prompts come from? How hard was it writing all those prompts! Where did the mechanic (the d10 and d6) and moving up and down the Prompt come from?

TH: Writing the Prompts and ensuring their variety was hard. I've been rewriting and refining them and realizing that it's something I could do for years and never be satisfied. The Prompts are a balance of learning about the vampire and how they relate to a constantly changing world, of bringing back the vampire's past to haunt them, and of resolving the horrific things the vampire might do because they are an awful vampire who sees humans as prey.

The Prompts have to be open-ended enough to apply to wherever and whenever a vampire is at a given moment. I've started vampire's in ancient Mesopotamia, Pictish Britain, 1300s France, and the prehistoric Indus River Valley and the Prompts are flexible enough to make sense in all those instances.

This isn't a generic game system, but the Prompts are very flexible.

To navigate the Prompts you subtract a d6 from a d10 and move forward or backward along the Prompt list that many entries. Each entry has two or three Prompts, you encounter the first entry the first time you land on that Prompt, the second entry if you land on it again, and so on. This let's a page of Prompt entries become a mini-story arc; the second entry builds on the first. This also creates an interesting probability spread because you'll only seldom encounter a third tier Prompt entry. This means that third tier entries can be gigantic and outrageous and change the story or the world dramatically and you'll only encounter one or two in a game so it doesn't feel overblown.

Answering Prompts is pretty easy. You are usually forced to gain or spend Resources or Skills in a Prompt description, so these give you good hooks to hang your narration on.

SH: You have mentioned baking spaces for queerness into some of the prompts. Could you talk a little bit about that and why you felt it was important to do so?

TH: I'm a cishet white guy, but I work in a world full of LGBTQA+ folks. Some Prompts make a space that can used as a point of thinking about queerness for people like me, I think.

SH: Do you find yourself drawn more to the Quick or Strolling version of the game? Have you had any feedback on preferences from play testers?

TH: I'm 100% a "Quick" player. I think that comes out of years of writing succinct *Burning Wheel* Beliefs. My main playtester is 100% in the other camp, though, and she's smart as heck so I'm not going to make doubtful sounds. Other playtesters seem mixed.

I think the most exciting possibility for the "Strolling" version is that players might write in their books like a Diary. That was the original intention before I realized the elegance of streamlined play.

SH: How have your experiences with Kickstarter shaped the way you design games? Is it a tool you use every time or only on selected project?

TH: I'm mostly making ridiculous little two or three page games I give away for free. There's no real way to package those, even if there was a demand, and that's fine because their best form is a free PDF. I do think that Kickstarter makes me realize that there is a possibility for a game to be realized if it's best form happens to be a book or a box or a carved piece of wood. It lets me think bigger and that's great.

The game renaissance that Kickstarter has kicked off is incredible and I can't thank the company enough for it.

SH: Do you have expectations for *Thousand Year Old Vampire* in terms of its success? More than just making its Kickstarter goal?

TH: Ergh. Honestly, I think that *Thousand Year Old Vampire* will meet the minimum goal that lets me produce a POD hardback book. I don't have the social media presence, the fan base, the advertising savvy, or enough friends to have it be a success by most measures. I'll be happy if I survive this with my dignity intact.

SH: Do you have a favorite vampire from literature or a favorite that you have created while playing the game?

TH: I really was affected by Ben Passmore's comic. I keep going back and rereading it. The vampire in the comic is a creature of senseless habit who can't tell mortals apart, and keeps running through the same cycles of need and accidental murder. It's fantastic.

Fictional characters that most influenced the way I think about this game are the ancient characters in *Adventure Time*—Princess Bubblegum, The Ice King, Marceline, and in the last episode BMO. Each of them have deeply fucked up ways of dealing with being ancient and they are rife with things that come back to haunt them. In the last episode of the series BMO gets Finn's name wrong and, oh man, that's just the most heartbreaking thing ever.

Thousand Year Old Vampire does a great job of stringing together three or four Prompts into a story arc that goes places. One instance that I just can't shake had a vampire who had been turned when he was a Roman caesar. He was ultimately forced to flee westward with a legion which devolved over generations into banditry on the Russian steppes.

Wherever he went a supernatural thundercloud cast a shadow over the region, letting him go about during the day. He negotiates a title by marrying a daughter of the Tsar who then betrays the vampire and tries to have him murdered. He and his new bride flee back into the steppes on the day of their wedding; there they find his wife Empress Augrina from centuries ago waiting, somehow now an immortal.

They all three go to the wedding bed together only to get a Prompt that a century passes and all mortals die. I decide that they go to sleep and waked up a century later, the Tsar's daughter a desiccated corpse. The next Prompt calls for confusion and madness and betrayal, so on a train the vampire is betrayed by his immortal former wife harms him grievously. The next Prompt is "You awaken covered in dust. Generations have passed. Your sleeping place has been sealed off. How do you escape? Lose a Resource." But I had no Resource or Skills left to spend, so that was the end of the vampire's journey. He lies there still, alive and conscious in a coffin deep beneath the earth

And this might be the greatest testament I can give my own gam It makes me want to do that most awful of all things—tell you abou my character.

SH: Tim, when does the Kicksta go live?

TH: The plan is to launch Oct 2 2018 at 10am PST.

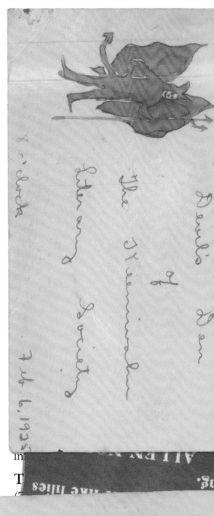

2. Log Rolling Contest
3. Hangman's Noose
4. Aerial Contest
5. Trip to Europe
6. Tongue Twister
7. Nerve Test
8. Calisthenics
9. Linger Longer
   Lingerie

away in carving can be used for all washing purpo
the soap which constitutes the final carving is actual
amount.

Appendix Five

Suggestions for Group Play

"Hacking" rules is a fundamental part of role-playing. It's part of the delight of gaming to take a system and break it gently until it's all yours because no one else wants those broken pieces of game crockery scattered all over the room. Even though *Thousand Year Old Vampire* is a solo game, it only takes a little work to modify it for simultaneous play with multiple players. Below, you will find suggestions for two different ways you might do this, designed to suit the Quick and Journaling modes of solo play.

The rules presented here are a loose guide to playing this game as a group--adjust them as needed. If you want to spend three hours role-playing out a scene in character, go ahead. Whatever you do, follow good game practices and make sure that everyone is having a fun, fruitful experience.

Journaling Games Take Days or Weeks

When playing as a group, the slower Journaling Game takes on an epistolary, or letter-writing, format. Whenever you generate a Prompt for your vampire, write your response as a letter to the other players instead of as a journal entry. Play happens simultaneously, although players will need to keep their vampires in similar timelines. If a big time jump occurs for one vampire the others will need to catch up. Maybe the remaining players make two or three rolls while they catch up to the character who has fallen asleep for a hundred years.

Quick Games Take a Few Hours

Quick Games work best when played at a table, face to face. No one is writing out long journal entries, so responses can be kept brief. The players keep their attention focused on whoever is taking a turn, showing their interest in the player and their character. You might want to allow subsequent players to roll for their Prompts in advance and think them through ahead of their turns.

In quick play, brevity is key. Players honor the intention of one-sentence Experiences by describing Prompt reactions in just a few lines. You shouldn't need to act out scenes; this isn't that kind of experience.

The larger the group, the slower you will progress through the list of Prompts. Consider rolling two d10s (instead of one) and subtracting the usual single d6. This will both speed up the game and prevent players from rolling the same Prompts again and again.

Time and geography are other considerations. If there is a big time jump during group quick play, each player can simply incorporate that hundred-year leap into their own narratives. It is also helpful to geographically reunite the vampires every couple of rounds by keeping them in adjacent towns or nearby regions where they can still interact with each other. Of course, physical separation becomes less important as modern transport and communications shrink once-great distances.

If someone rolls a Prompt that has already been encountered by another player, progress to the first new entry within that Prompt. So, if one player encountered the first entry in the Prompt, the next player who rolled that Prompt would skip the first entry and instead encounter the second. These vampires may or may not share the narrative arc of the entries in that prompt--it's up to their players and what makes sense.

General Multiplayer Rules

Both game formats encourage players to gently push and pull at each other. Part of the way this works is through sharing Characters and Resources.

When initially creating your group of vampires, they should be geographically close to the others and should each have a relationship to one other vampire at the table. One of my vampire's Characters, the chief sapper in the army of an Assyrian general, could be romantically entangled with the general's heir--who happens to be another player's vampire. Creating interconnections between Characters like this helps the group flesh out the relationships between their own vampires and provides them something to reminisce about in three or four hundred years.

Characters may be given an additional relationship with another player's vampire every time a Prompt causes an interaction with the character. For example, early in the game I create Brecht, an American Civil War veteran. He stokes the fire at the Antarctic retreat, and in a later Prompt I determine that Brecht stole my Diary. In that subsequent Prompt I create a connection between Brecht and another vampire with Searching Brecht's rooms I find a tintype of the dread Piancastelli; what does this mean? Players should agree on these kinds of connections, unless, of course, everyone agrees not to agree.

Any Character, regardless of who created them, can be tapped by any player to satisfy a Character requirement in a Prompt. Characters aren't owned by any one player, but it is best to pay attention to when players are invested in a Character and would prefer they weren't murdered without good reason.

Resources can move between vampires, too. If a Prompt instructs a player to gain a Resource, that player can elect to take a Resource from another player's vampire. Optionally, when told to lose a Resource a player may choose to steal a Resource from another vampire. Roll a d6: on a 1-3, the thief gains the Resource; on a 4-6, the stolen Resource is lost to both vampires but still satisfies the 'lose a Resource' requirement from the Prompt.

APPENDIX SIX
PLAY EXAMPLES

Example One

I think I want to create a vampire in early Eastern Europe, so I look up names and choose Ada. Next, I decide Ada is a Slav living in the region that will later become Poland. I start her first Memory with one Experience that encapsulates Ada's existence up to this point: *I am Ada, a Slavic woman living on the edge of the wild Tatra Mountains.*

I choose some Traits for Ada.

Characters:
Piotr, a shepherd boy who tends my flocks
Róża, my elderly mother, she lives in my homestead
Hania, my neighbor, a friend and enemy

Skills:
Gentle Butcher
Beermaking
Hill Wanderer

Resources:
Ornate Walking Staff
Large Flock of Sheep
Sack of Silver Coins

WITHDRAWN

Then I combine these Traits to create three new Memories, each containing one Experience.

All day, Mother Róża sits quietly by the beer vat; she says it sings sweet songs to her, and she carves what she hears onto a magnificent ash walking stick.
Piotr was orphaned during a bandit raid; I hold his family's silver coin until he comes of age–in the meantime he works with the sheep.
Hania complains when I walk my sheep through the stream, but she never says no to the mutton I gift her.

Next I create another Character: the vampire who will cast Ada into unlife, along with a Mark and a Memory related to this.

Character: *Vyri, a stick-thin thing that lives in a cave*

Memory: *Wandering through the hills, I hear someone crying for help; it is a trick by the demon Vyri, who drinks my blood then casts me into a mountain stream to die–Hania and her husband pull me from the water hours later, thinking me dead.*

Mark: *Skin like ice; I am careful not to touch anyone*

I now have a vampire composed of three Skills, three Resources, one Mark, and five Memories made up of one Experience each. I'm ready for Ada to start encountering Prompts.

I roll a d10 and a d6, subtracting the latter from the former. I get an 8 and a 3: 8 minus 3 is 5. Starting at Prompt 1, I count forward five Prompts to Prompt 6: "A mortal Character begins serving you. Who are they? Why are they drawn to you? Create a new mortal Character."

Let's see... The first thing that comes to mind is pretty wild. I create *Josse, an astronomer of the French court.* I need to write an Experience about him and attach it to one of Ada's Memories. To the second Memory, the one about Piotr, I add, *These same bandits bring me Josse, a ragged wanderer who tells me in halting Polish that he foresaw my rise to mystic power in the stars and has been searching for me for five years; he installs himself in an outbuilding and makes intricate masks out of river clay.*

One sentence answers are the limit, even if they get stretchy.

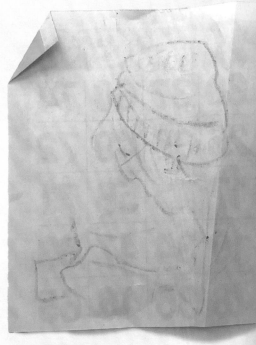

Soo-ae is a Korean-born vampire who we find in 1855 living on a whaling station in Greenland. Soo-ae is currently at Prompt 56 and they have had many, many things happen during their long existence; all five of their Memories are full, containing three Experiences each.

Rolling a 1, Soo-ae progresses to Prompt 57: "Your knowledge of old things becomes a strength. Based on a checked Skill what knowledge do you share with contemporary mortals? Check a Skill. Create a Resource."

Oh, neat! I think that Soo-ae's time in Britain in the service of Queen Eltilda the Brave, hundreds of years ago, gave them insight into complex issues of inheritance and title. They have the checked Skill *Sea Lawyer*, which relates closely enough.

Soo-ae only has two unchecked Skills: *Biting Wit* and *Sled Dog Trainer*. Dang, this is tough. I strike out *Biting Wit* and start to write an Experience.

That's when I realize Soo-ae's five Memory slots are all full up with three Experiences each, and their Diary is also full with four Memories containing three Experiences each. I strike out a Memory from Soo-ae's Diary about traveling the Silk Road with their father five hundred years ago and move one of their current Memories into the book. Soo-ae no longer has any Memories relating to their time before becoming a vampire.

In the newly freed Memory slot I write, *I become a correspondent with the London magazine* Punch*; my barbed poems about the histories of prominent families reveal that I know much, and they are soon hiring me to both share secrets and keep them.*

Lastly, I take the Resource *A Fat London Bank Account.*

ANGELUS
NOVUS
from mona

Appendix VII

What is a Role-playing Game?

The single most *crucial* thing in the understanding of games

of *St. Augustine* were only the

SECOND SIG

OR, THE

POLMOSCOPIAN

This feat will put to blush the land
"————dire magicians throw their mi
And wise men walked as on enchanted

lown: Roleplay... games are
... playing a rol... ...laying a
... ...es as ...ou were the
..., ...d ... ...me to be
... ...ot just a game where
... ... f the
...
...sic

13. 7. 37.

ČESKO-SLOVENSKO
5K

Socialist Party,
N e w   Y o r k , 10, N.Y.
303 Fourth Ave.
U S A.

ÚSTŘEDNÍ SEKRETARIÁT ČESKOSLOVENSKÉ SOCIÁLNÍ DEMOKRACIE V PRAZE
PRAHA I, PŘÍKOPY 25, TELEFON 237-41

New York

...oung so make
...atement:
...ssociated me-
...re not roleplay.

Fold me.

Appendix VIII

Game Design, Layout, and Collage: Tim Hutchings
Lead Brainstormer/Playtester: Jessie Rainbow
Editor: Dr. Melody Watson
Additional Editing: Dr. Ezra Claverie
Additional Prompts: Elizabeth Bellisario
                                   Amber Autumn Faebrooke
                                   Jessie Rainbow
                                   Jackson Tegu
Graphic Design Consultation: Sarah Doombringer
Add'l Graphic Design Consultation: Roman Gheesling
Cultural Consultants: Mariam Ahmad
                                   James Mendez Hodes
Safety Tools   Tayler Stokes

A special thanks to:
Pedro Amador-Gates
Andreas Marckmann Andreassen
Aura Belle
Marshall Bradshaw
Luke Crane & Kickstarter
Nathanial Elder
Jonathan Gilmour
Metatopia
Jason Morningstar
Ben Passmore
Janeanne Rockwell-Kincanon
Brie Sheldon
Daniel Wood

Image sources include:
The British Library
Hamersly Library, Western Oregon University
The State Archives of North Carolina
The National Archives of the U.S.A.

Thanks to these early reviewers:
Big Gay Nerds
Chimerical Realm
EN World
Game State
Man vs. Meeple
Roll for Crit
Shut Up & Sit Down
Tabletop Anarchy
Thoughty

pět
nná
hou
ylo
vit,
na,
ou

printed by McNaughton & Gunn in the USA

A tim hutchings game produced by Petite Guignol LLC

2019

Appendix Nine

A Character Record

This is a game to play in a notebook, or on a large white wall, or on a scroll ancient and lengthy, or maybe you will incise the words into a field of mud using a pointed stick. Record your character however you like.

Just know it's not practical to use a single sheet of paper because your vampire's Memories will quickly outgrow it. Nonetheless, on the next page you'll find a character sheet.

Do with it what you will.

A dedicated character sheet does have other uses. It might help you organize your own character sheet, or it could prove a key to understanding the game better, or it gives you an excuse to steal photocopies at work. It's all good.

The most practical and least thematically appropriate method of tracking a vampire is the one I use: I play in front of a computer and use a word processor. It's easy and efficient.

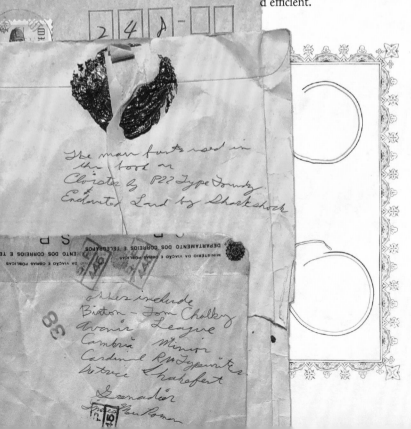

Memories

(Five Memories made of up to three Experiences ea

Diary

(Four Memories may be marked with a D for Diary)

Skills

Resources

Characters

Marks

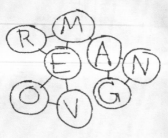

The core of this game came together in just a couple of days, powered by Mountain Dew and looping Tubeway Army. A crystallizing moment for my design process was re-reading Ben Passmore's comic short, "The Vampire." Passmore's titular character is a confused predator-thing steeped in occult arts—a mix of terrifying and pathetic, with a beaten up old beige computer in a shitty apartment.

It was sad and terrifying. I wanted to make a game that explored the space between Passmore's vampire and the casual, many-storied ancientness of characters like Marceline, the Ice King, Princess Bubblegum, and BMO in the show *Adventure Time.*

I'm excited about vampires that are incredibly old. They've lived many lives, had many names. They are in the process of losing their humanity as everything becomes patterns and habits. Their identities must change to fit the mutable world around them. Players of this game will make hard choices as their vampire forgets their homeland, their parents, their first love—all so they can understand how to buy tickets to ride on these newfangled locomotives.

The Diary mechanic ties directly to my own fears as an artist and archivist. If things are written down they can be lost; if they aren't written down they will be forgotten. Losing a diary or a sketchbook or notebook is like losing part of your own brain and I'm glad that conceit works as well as it does in this game. The Diary mechanic might have been suggested by Jessie Rainbow. Thank you!

The Memory mechanics owe a debt to *Burning Wheel's* Beliefs and Freemarket's memory system. The storytelling Prompt structure comes from a handful of disparate sources, with one of the most unexpected being solo war games that allow for emergent storytelling—games like B-17 and a NASA simulator from the 80s. These are games I've never played, but for which I have some sort of misplaced nostalgia. There's also a healthy dollop of a mental exercise I play sometimes: "how do you describe an eternity?"

This whole project was supposed to happen quickly but it looks like it has taken the game over a